A LOST GIRL'S GUIDE HOME

Awakening the Daughter of The King
A Devotional

By
Jessica Galaxy

Edited by
Micaela Heckman

WAYFOLK
PRESS

To Gabbie and Sky—
Sunshine and Starlight.
My song and my poem.

"... narrow is the road that leads to life, and only a few find it."
— Matthew 7:14

Table of Contents

1
Dear Lost Girl

I pray this letter finds you in time, for you are in grave danger. You may want to sit down, because what I'm about to tell you may be unsettling. This may be hard to believe—in fact, it's probably going to sound absolutely crazy—so I'm just going to say it: You are, indeed, a real-life, modern-day, completely for real... princess. (Extreme sigh of relief)

There. I said it.

I told you it would sound crazy, but I promise you, it's all true!

You are really the daughter of a King—and not just any King... but THE KING. The King of Lights, to be exact. Also known as the Majesty above majesties, the guy in charge, the Man upstairs, the Creator Himself... yeah, that guy. He's your dad. Your *Ultimate Dad*.

The man that you've been calling your dad is your earthly dad. Some earthly dads are good, and some aren't... but more on that later. Anyway, let's get back on track. The point I'm trying to make is that you were formed and crafted by your Father, The King, for His glory. I mean, your entire existence was designed with the intention to display the beauty of His goodness.

Now, I know you may be saying to yourself, "No way! This is ridiculous! The daughter of an all-powerful King? Me, a princess? Yeah, right! If I'm a princess of light, then why don't I shine or live in a castle... and how come I've never met this kingly Father of mine?"

These are all good questions—and I promise that I will do my best to answer, in detail, every one.

But the short answer, to sum them all up, is that a long time ago, an evil dragon—yes, a real dragon—stole your crown and put you in a deep, enchanted sleep.

How did he do this, you might ask?

Well, this sinister serpent deceived you into eating THE FORBIDDEN FRUIT of DARKNESS. Keep in mind that your Father, The King of Lights, is the opposite of darkness. So, by eating the forbidden fruit, The Dragon basically separated you from your Father.

I know this is a lot to take in, and you probably have a million questions like, "What in the world is this weird fruit-of-darkness tree doing in the orchard of The King of Lights in the first place?"

I know—it's a bit strange when you look at it that way.

But the fact of the matter is that the fruit itself had no power at all. It wasn't evil or dark or eerie-looking—nothing like that. You might even say it was no different than your average apple.

You see, it was the choice to obey that held the real power. Your Father commanded you not to eat from that tree, and He gave you the free will to choose to obey Him or not. For love always gives a choice. And your Father—well, He *is* Love, and He loves you more than you could ever imagine.

So the ultimate being of Love gave the ultimate choice... and He stacked the odds in your favor, planting thousands of good fruit trees and only forbidding one. He made it easy to choose His goodness and pointless to want what is bad, placing the curse as far away from your desires as possible.

And since the ultimate being of Love gave you the ultimate choice to obey, the consequence of disobedience would separate you from Him... ultimately.

The Dragon knew this, and he used it against you. For when you least expected it, he sneaked into your Father's orchard and whispered into your ear a lie that would change your life forever.

In a nutshell, he told you that if you ate from the forbidden tree, you would not slip into darkness. Instead, your eyes would be opened and you would be as powerful as The King of Lights. He tempted you with the pleasure of its taste, the beauty of its shape, and the fame of its power.

For instead of powerful, the fruit made you weak—stripping away your royal crown and forcing you into an enchanted slumber inside the dream world of Dystopia, where you now reside.

So you see... The Dragon lied.

The purpose of this guide is to help you wake up and find your way home. There are many obstacles and traps in the world of Dystopia. Use this guide to help you find The Way Road, and once you find it, do not turn from it for any reason.

For it is the only way back to your Father.

I will be in touch throughout your journey whenever you need my help. Don't worry, just trust your Dad and you'll be back home in no time.

Sincerely,

The Helper

2
Your Tool Box

Every princess in a battle needs two things: a crown and tools

You weren't dropped into this world to just survive it. You were called to walk through it, stand in it, and fight when needed. And your Father didn't leave you empty-handed.

Welcome to your toolbox.
Inside are the essentials: prayer, the Sword (aka, your Bible), and faith. These aren't spiritual accessories—they're survival gear. They help you hear from The King, fight back lies, and stay standing when everything else is falling apart. This chapter is where we open it up—one tool at a time.

You've got a journey ahead. Let's make sure you're equipped.

Tool # 1
Your Shield of Faith

Let's talk about faith. The word alone probably makes your eyes glaze over. Like—okay cool, I've heard that before. Faith. Got it. Trust God. Whatever.

But here's the thing: if you don't understand what faith really is, you'll miss the very thing that can wake you up and get you home.

Because faith isn't just an idea. It's the shield that pushes through the attacks of Dystopia. It's the key that unlocks the castle gates. It's what connects you to the only One who can break the curse.

And no, it's not about "believing in yourself." (That's a cute social media quote, but not what saves your soul.) There are two kinds of faith you need on this journey. One saves your life. The other helps you live it.

Let's break it down, shall we?

Saving Faith:
Trusting the One Your Father Sent

Once upon a time (aka: the beginning of literally everything), you were made to walk in the light. You were royalty—crowned, covered, completely known and loved by The King of Lights.

Then the serpent came. (Ugh. Him again.) He tricked you. He fed you lies. And the curse? It hit hard. Shame entered. Fear crept in. The world cracked.

And the only thing that could fix it... was a Savior.
Enter Jesus. The real one. Not "Sunday school Jesus" with the sheep and the nice quotes. But The White Knight Jesus. The one who came into Dystopia, fought The Dragon, and laid His life down to break the curse—for you.

Faith begins when you stop trying to rescue yourself and admit that He's your only way out. Saving faith isn't about being good. It's about trusting the One who already is.
You don't earn it. You receive it.

So if you've never really said it out loud—if you've never told Jesus, "I believe You're the only way back to my Father"... please, say it now. That's where the light begins.

Scripture Anchor:
For it is by grace you have been saved, through faith—and this is not from yourselves, it is the gift of God."
(Ephesians 2:8)

9

Keeping Faith:
Holding On When Weary

So here's the awkward part people often leave out: life doesn't magically become a fairy tale once you accept the gift of the Savior (Jesus, The White Knight). There's no dramatic music cue, no glittery castle, no get-there-quick fun montage. There's just you trusting God, day to day.

Yes, you believe. You're in. You love God. But now what? Suddenly you're stuck waiting for your happily ever after, but in order to get there—you still have to get through this wild, messy world. Unless the Rapture comes first... more on that later.

The point is: how do you walk like a daughter of The King after the mountaintop glow fades? How do you keep the crown on straight when the Wi-Fi's lagging, your prayers feel like echoes, and Dystopia's throwing flaming lies at your head? Well... this is where *keeping faith* comes in.

What's Keeping faith?

It's what happens after the mountaintop moment—when the glory settles and real life attacks.

It's the "God, I don't see You, but I'm still trusting You" kind of faith. When you can praise in the pain, sing through the suffering, and trust through the tears.

It's not loud. It's not fancy. It's not always inspirational. But it *is* powerful.

You don't have to feel it. You don't have to see it. You just have to keep walking, limping—even crawling—one prayer, one scripture, one decision at a time.

Keeping faith is saying yes to God in the middle of the mess. It's trusting He's still good when everything around you looks like chaos. It's staying close to Him—even when your emotions are doing backflips. It's not always faith like a feast. Rather, it's often faith like a scared, fragile, unhinged seed.

And guess what? Even that small, fragile seed of faith counts. It counts a lot, actually. Because seeds grow into big things.

Scripture Anchor:
"... if you have faith as a mustard seed, you will say to this mountain, 'Move from here to there,' and it will move; and nothing will be impossible for you." (Matthew 17:20)

Points to Ponder: The Faith Journey

- Have I ever really put my faith in Jesus to rescue me—or have I just been trying to be "good enough" on my own?

- What lies are trying to shake my faith in this season?

- Do I only trust God when things feel easy—or am I learning to walk with Him in the dark too?

- What's one step of faith I can take today, even if I don't feel ready?

Let's Bring It In

Faith isn't a feeling. It's not a spiritual filter or a churchy checklist. It's the rope that pulls you out of the pit. It's the key to the door that opens to the path home—to your Savior and your Father.
Saving faith says, "Jesus, You're my only way home."

Keeping faith says, "I still trust You—right here, right now."
You don't have to get it perfect. You just have to start.

Tool # 2
Your Father's Sword aka
The Bible

Life feels like a battle some days. Between the pressure and the chaos, it's easy to feel lost. But your Father didn't leave you empty-handed. He gave you a sword—aka, the Bible.

It's not just a good book. It's your weapon and your compass. But it won't help if you don't pick it up.

Let's break it down, shall we?

Protection for When the Enemy Attacks

Make no mistake—the enemy isn't passive. He stalks. He schemes. And he's got one mission: steal your identity, your purpose, and your connection to your Father.

But your Father didn't just give you light to walk by—He gave you a sword to fight with.

The Word of God is your defense and your offense. When lies roar, you respond with truth. When fear lunges, you hold steady—because you know Who holds you.

This isn't metaphorical fluff. This is warfare. Spiritual attacks don't always look like demons and fire. Sometimes they look like late-night spirals, comparison loops, or that one voice in your head that says, "You're not enough."

But The Word slices through the enemy's whispers and reminds you of what's true: You are loved. You are chosen. You are not alone.

Scripture Anchor:
"As for God, His way is perfect; The word of the Lord is proven; He is a shield to all who trust in Him." (Psalm 18:30)

Guidance Through the Jungle

In a world like ours, confusion isn't rare—it's normal. You're told to trust your feelings, follow your heart, and binge whatever makes you "feel good." But what happens when your feelings lie? What happens when your favorite show makes you numb to stuff that should bother you? When the music makes pain sound poetic instead of something to heal?

That's where the Sword comes in.

God's Word doesn't just make you FEEL better—it also makes you SEE better. It clears the emotional fog. It slices through the noise. It helps you recognize when your emotions are spiraling, when your anger is louder than your peace, when your comfort tv-show is secretly feeding your anxiety.

The Bible doesn't say, "Don't feel things."
It says, "Here's how to feel things truthfully."

When your anxiety says, "You're not safe,"
The Word says, "God is your refuge."

When your pride says, "Snap back—get even,"
The Word says, "Be slow to anger. Be quick to forgive."

When your favorite playlist says, "Just give up,"
The Word says, "God has a plan for your life."

This isn't about rules—it's about rescue.
God's Word doesn't cut you down. It cuts through the
mess—so you can finally see clearly and walk freely.

Scripture Anchor:

"For the word of God is living and powerful, and sharper than
any two-edged sword, piercing even to the division of soul
and spirit, and of joints and marrow, and is a discerner of the
thoughts and intents of the heart." (Hebrews 4:12)

Points to Ponder

- Are there shows, songs, or social media voices shaping how I think more than God's Word is?

- When was the last time I used Scripture to fact-check my feelings?

- If the Bible is a sword that cuts through confusion, what's one lie I need it to slice down this week?

Let's Bring It In

Your Father didn't leave you wandering or defenseless. He gave you a sword—His Word—and it's sharper than anything this world can throw at you. When the path is overgrown with lies and confusion, the Bible cuts through and shows you what's real. When your emotions twist the truth, it steadies you. When the enemy whispers that you're unworthy, alone, or too far gone, it answers back with power.

The Bible isn't just paper and ink. It is a weapon forged in heaven, placed in your hands by the God who loves you. Let it guide you. Let it protect you. And when you don't know what to do—let it speak.

Tool # 3
Prayer: Your Direct Line

Hey, Princess, grab your crown and lean in close—we're talking about one of the most powerful tools in your royal arsenal: PRAYER. It's not just a hotline to heaven; it's your direct, uninterrupted, always-on connection to The King. Think of it as the reconnected line to your Father, the ultimate way to stay close to Him, and a secret weapon to fight The Dragon and his sneaky schemes.

Let's break it down, shall we?

Prayer is Your Direct Line to The King

Imagine picking up your phone, dialing The King's private number, and hearing His voice on the other end: "I'm here, my child. What's on your heart?" Well...that's exactly what prayer is—a royal conversation with the One who knows you better than anyone else.

You don't need fancy words or perfect timing. Just talk to Him. Share your joys, your fears, your dreams, and even your messy, unfiltered thoughts. He's always listening.

And that's because The King isn't just a ruler on a throne; He's your Dad, and He loves when you hang out with Him. When you pray, you're building your relationship with Him. You're learning to recognize His voice, feel His presence, and understand His heart.

 *Scripture Anchor:*
"Now this is the confidence that we have in Him, that if we ask anything according to His will, He hears us." (1 John 5:14)

Prayer is a Weapon Against The Dragon

Now, let's talk strategy. The Dragon? He's not just lurking around for fun—he's actively trying to mess with your journey. But guess what? You've got a weapon that sends him running: prayer. When you pray, you're not just talking to The King; you're inviting Him to step into the battle. And trust me, when The King fights, The Dragon loses.
Every. Single. Time.

Prayer has magical power to bind the invisible agents of the enemy. Feeling attacked by fear, doubt, or lies? Pray. Trust me—The King will send His heavenly warriors to protect you and push back the darkness. The Dragon hates it when you pray because he knows it cuts off his influence and reminds you of your authority as The King's daughter.

Which is why he will do everything in his power to keep your mouth shut. But don't let him! Open your mouth and SPEAK!

Scripture Anchor:
"Is anyone among you suffering? Let him pray. Is anyone cheerful? Let him sing psalms." (James 5:13)

Prayer Changes You

Here's a secret about prayer: it doesn't just change your circumstances—it changes you. Spending time in prayer helps you see the world through The King's eyes. It strengthens your faith, fills your heart with peace, and reminds you of who you are. When you pray, you're aligning your heart with His. And that alignment? It's what gives you the courage to keep walking The Way Road.

Scripture Anchor:
"...The earnest prayer of a righteous person has great power and produces wonderful results." (James 5:16)

19

Points to Ponder: How to Pray Like Royalty

- Are you being real with God, or trying to sound "holy"? What would it look like to just speak from the heart?

- Are you willing to keep praying even when answers don't come right away? Can you trust that The King still hears you?

- What are you thankful for today? Can you start your prayer by naming a few of those things?

- What bold thing do you want to ask for? Are you holding back when The King's power is limitless?

- When was the last time you stopped to listen in prayer? What might God be saying if you paused long enough to hear?

Let's Bring It In

Princess, prayer isn't just a tool; it's your lifeline. It connects you to The King, strengthens your spirit, and reminds you that you're never alone. Whether you're whispering a quick prayer in the middle of chaos or spending quiet moments pouring out your heart, every word you speak matters. The King hears, The Helper intercedes, and The Dragon trembles.

So, pick up the line and call your Father. He's waiting to hear your voice. And trust me—He's got plenty to say back.

The Way Road

Hello, Princess. Welcome to the most important part of your story—the journey back home. You've probably heard of epic quests before: brave knights, daring escapes, and treacherous paths leading to faraway kingdoms. But let me tell you, nothing compares to The Way Road. This is no ordinary path. It's the one-and-only road that leads you out of Dystopia and back to The Kingdom of Lights.

And here's the amazing part: The Way Road wasn't just discovered—it was made. It was paved by the sacrifice of The White Knight, Jesus. So, it's a road unlike any other. It's straight, it's narrow, and yes, it's filled with challenges. But here's the best news: it's already finished. The White Knight's victory ensures that if you follow The Way Road, you will make it home. Let's explore what makes this road so extraordinary.

Let's break it down, shall we?

The Road is Made of Love

Let's Recap: You were trapped in Dystopia, all tangled up in lies, weighed down by guilt, and surrounded by darkness. There was no way out—at least, not one you could make on your own. But then, The White Knight stepped in. He didn't just point to a way of escape; He became the way of escape. By His sacrifice, He cleared the path and opened the gates so you could find your way home.

This road? It's paved with His love for you. Every stone, every step is a reminder that He chose you, fought for you, and gave everything to bring you back to The Kingdom. Walking The Way Road isn't about earning your place; it's about accepting the gift that's already been given.

Scripture Anchor:

"Jesus said to him, 'I am the way, and the truth, and the life. No one comes to the Father except through me.'" (John 14:6)

The Road is Narrow (But Worth It)

The Way Road isn't the most popular path. It's not wide or flashy, and it's definitely not lined with glittery shortcuts. It's narrow, and at times, it can feel lonely. But here's the thing—it's the only road that leads to The Kingdom. Every other path? Dead ends, traps, or worse... straight into The Dragon's lair.

Walking this road means saying no to distractions and yes to The King's call. It means trusting His guidance even when the world around you screams otherwise. But don't let the narrowness scare you—the destination is worth every step.

Scripture Anchor:
"Enter by the narrow gate. For the gate is wide and the way is easy that leads to destruction, and those who enter by it are many. (Matthew 7:13-14)

The Road is Lit & Protected

Walking The Way Road won't shield you from battle—but it does guarantee the war has already been won. The Dragon still circles, roaring threats, laying traps, and whispering that you're too broken to belong. But don't be deceived. This road is not just a path—it's a battlefield already claimed. The White Knight didn't just clear the way; He conquered it. With His blood, He marked every step as holy ground. No enemy can lay siege to what He's secured.

So stand your ground. Fix your eyes on the One who went before you. Keep marching—not because *you're* strong, but because the ground beneath your feet *is*. I'm here—The Helper—walking beside you, guarding, whispering courage when the fire rises. And above it all, The King watches. Not distant. Not idle. But with eyes blazing and heart fierce, He calls you forward. Every step you take brings you closer to home... and closer to Him.

Scripture Anchor:
"And behold, I am with you always, to the end of the age."
(Matthew 28:20)

Points to Ponder

- If the way is narrow, am I willing to walk it when no one else around me is? Or am I drawn to the comfort of crowds and the illusion of ease?

- Do I remember that this road was paved with love and sacrifice? When I get tired or discouraged, do I walk like it cost Him everything?

- Do I trust that this road is protected—even when I feel attacked or afraid? Or do I forget the victory that's already been won?

- Am I leaning on The Helper, or trying to muscle through on my own? Do I pause to listen, to let Him guide and strengthen me?

- Am I tempted to step off the Way for something quicker, easier, or more accepted? And if so... what lies am I believing about where that road leads?

Let's Bring It In

Princess, The Way Road isn't just a path—it's a promise. A promise that no matter how far you've wandered or how lost you've felt, there is a way home. The White Knight made sure of that. So step forward, one foot in front of the other, and let the journey begin. The Kingdom awaits.

3
About the Opposition

You're not just walking through life—
you're walking through a war.

The Dragon, his demons, and this twisted world have set traps all around you. And just when you think it's all outside noise, you find out they've got an inside man. But don't worry—we're about to pull back the curtain and show you who's really running this fight.

Know Your Enemy

Let's get one thing straight: The Dragon? The serpent? The devil? ... He. Hates. Your. Guts. Not in the "ugh, she's annoying" way. No, I mean full-blown, scorched-earth, no-mercy, all hate kind of way.

And it's not even personal—well, not directly.
It's more so about your Father. Your heavenly one: The King of Lights... and the love He has for you.

Let's break it down, shall we?

A Beautiful Start Gone Bitter

Once upon a time, long before you were born, your Father made a powerful being named Lucifer. He was beautiful. Bright. A creature of music and light. But he wasn't made in the image of God. And that would have been fine... until he saw you.

Lucifer wanted more. His jealousy and anger caused his heart to sin, and he tried to take your Father's throne. He actually started a war in heaven (him and the angels that were foolish enough to come against your Dad).

In the end, they all got the boot. Which landed them here... on Earth. How'd you think it got like this?!

Now he's a bitter shadow of who he once was. His beauty? Twisted. His power? Fading. His mission? To destroy whatever The King loves most. Which includes you... especially you.

Because unlike him, you were made in the Father's image. Unlike him, you were chosen to be an heir. You get the love, the crown, the inheritance, the name. You get the place in your Father's Kingdom that The Dragon always wanted.

And for that... he hates you and wants you obliterated.

Scripture Anchor:

"Stay alert! Watch out for your great enemy, the devil. He prowls around like a roaring lion, looking for someone to devour." (1 Peter 5:8)

27

Satan: Your Primary Opponent

Now that you know who your enemy is, you must understand that he will stop at nothing to destroy you. He will craft lies, set traps, and tempt you with the most beautiful poison. It is a hatred that surpasses insanity. Think fairytale villain with real-life danger.

That's why he's built this whole Dystopian world—to keep you asleep and separated from your Father forever.

The Bible calls him many names: Satan, the deceiver, the accuser, The Dragon. But no matter what you call him, just know—he's already lost. Jesus crushed him at the cross. And while the enemy may still roar, his power has been stripped. He has no authority over a daughter who knows who her Father is.

But here's the thing: he's sneaky. He doesn't show up with horns and a pitchfork. He whispers. He flatters. He blends in with the noise. He makes darkness look fun, sin look harmless, and lies sound kinda poetic.

So stay sharp. Know who your enemy is—and more importantly, know that he's already been defeated.

 *Scripture Anchor:*
"And no wonder! For Satan himself transforms himself into an angel of light." (2 Corinthians 11:14)

Demons: Satan's Henchmen

They're not just creepy shadows or characters from a scary movie—demons are real. They're Satan's flunkies, the ones who followed him when he rebelled against God. Total traitors.

Some are strong, sure—but none of them are stronger than your Dad, Princess. Not even close. Their mission? To hurt, distract, and confuse you.

But you weren't left defenseless. You've got your sword in hand (The Word). Your shield of faith on your arm, and a direct line to Heaven through prayer. You're not fighting alone. So stand tall, armor up, and don't be scared of the dark—they should be scared of *you*.

 ## Scripture Anchor:
"Finally, my brethren, be strong in the Lord and in the power of His might. Put on the whole armor of God, that you may be able to stand against the wiles of the devil." (Ephesians 6:10-11)

29

Points to Ponder

- What lies has the enemy been whispering to me lately?

- Am I taking the enemy seriously, or treating him like a cartoon?

- Do I recognize the difference between conviction from God and shame from the enemy?

- What weapons has God already given me to fight back?

Let's Bring It In

You have an enemy—but he's not stronger than your Father. He's not more powerful than your Savior. And, with the Helper on your side, the enemy better get used to defeat.

Because you're not fighting *for* victory... You're fighting *from* victory. So stand firm. Stay alert. Speak the truth. And when you get tired? Just remember—your Father has never lost a battle. And He never will.

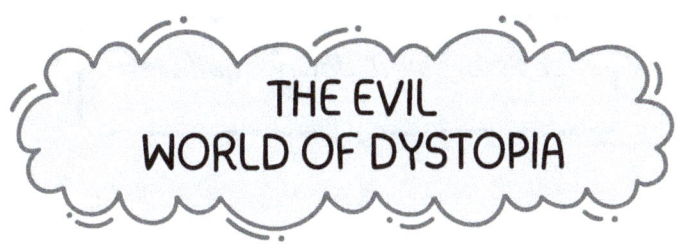

THE EVIL
WORLD OF DYSTOPIA

Welcome to Dystopia, Princess—a land where everything looks shiny on the surface but reeks of lies underneath. Imagine The Dragon as a shady real estate agent, selling you on "luxury living" in a world that's nothing more than a glittery dumpster-fire. The buildings? Crooked and crumbling. The skies? Always gray, like the background of a dystopian video game. And the people? They're enchanted too—trapped in their own slumber, chasing mirages of happiness that disappear as soon as they get close.

This isn't your home. Dystopia is a cheap knockoff of the beautiful world your Father created for you. The Dragon, in all his arrogance, took what was good and twisted it into something dark, convincing everyone it's normal.

But deep down, you know something's off. You feel it when you watch TV, scroll on social media, or listen to the world's soundtrack. Everything here is designed to keep you asleep, distracted, and as far away from your Father as possible.

> *Let's break it down, shall we?*

It's a Rigged Game

Living in Dystopia is like playing a video game where The Dragon wrote the code—and spoiler alert, he cheats. The music you hear, the shows you binge, the ads you scroll past —they're all part of his strategy. He wants you to stay stuck chasing after things that will never fulfill you: fame, money, or validation from others. It's a rigged game where the "prizes" only lead to more emptiness.

Think about it: have you ever felt that weird hollow feeling after spending hours on social media? That's Dystopia working its magic. The Dragon whispers, "Just one more scroll, one more click, and you'll finally feel satisfied." But it's all a lie. He's setting up traps disguised as shiny distractions, pulling you deeper into the wasteland.

The King's truth reminds you: "Do not love the world or the things in the world" (1 John 2:15). You're not made to fit into this broken system. Your Father designed you for something so much greater.

Scripture Anchor:
"The world and its desires pass away, but whoever does the will of God lives forever." (1 John 2:17)

The Glitter Isn't Gold

Dystopia thrives on its ability to make the fake look fabulous. Everything here is wrapped in shiny packaging, from the glamorous lifestyles on TV to the endless parade of "perfect" photos online. Your enemy can make a pile of garbage look like a birthday gift.

But once you peel back the glitter, you'll see the cracks. That "perfect" influencer? They're usually struggling with insecurity. That super-popular girl in school everyone wants to be? Half the time, she's exhausted from pretending.

The Dragon loves to sell you the illusion of happiness, but it always comes at a price. He doesn't care about your joy—he cares about keeping you stuck. Don't trust him.

Scripture Anchor:
"And what do you benefit if you gain the whole world but lose your own soul? Is anything worth more than your soul?" (Matthew 16:26)

Scripture Anchor:
"Just as death and destruction are never satisfied, so human desire is never satisfied." (Proverbs 27:20)

Who Are You Becoming Here?

Dystopia isn't just a place—it's a system designed to shape you. Every decision you make here, every influence you let in, is pulling you closer to *someone*. The question is, *who*?
Are you becoming more like The King, reflecting His love, truth, and grace? Or are you starting to blend into Dystopia—chasing its glittery lies, speaking its language, and forgetting who you really are? Think about the choices you've made recently. Are they leading you closer to home, or deeper into the wasteland?

Who Are You Becoming?

This isn't about guilt—it's about awareness. The Dragon loves when you move through life on autopilot, not noticing how Dystopia is shaping your heart and mind. But your Father calls you to wake up, to see the world clearly and to choose intentionally.

The beauty of being a daughter of The King is that you're never too far gone. No matter how long you've wandered in Dystopia, the moment you turn back to Him, He's ready to guide you home. So, Princess, take a moment to reflect: Who am I becoming in this world, and is it who I want to be?

Scripture Anchor:
"Don't copy the behavior and customs of this world, but let God transform you into a new person by changing the way you think. Then you will learn to know God's will for you, which is good and pleasing and perfect." (Romans 12:2)

Points to Ponder

- What lies has Dystopia sold you? Reflect on the promises this world makes and how they've left you feeling empty.

- Are you being shaped by The Dragon or The King? Think about how your daily choices are influencing the person you're becoming.

- What would your Father say about your path? Consider whether your actions and priorities reflect His heart or the distractions of Dystopia.

- How can you reflect The King's love here? Even in the darkness, your light can point others to the truth.

Let's Bring It In

Dystopia may be dark and broken, but it's not your home, Princess. You're not defined by the lies, distractions, or traps The Dragon sets. You're a daughter of The King, called to walk in truth and light, even in the middle of the mess.

The next time Dystopia whispers its glittery lies, pause and remember: The King has already given you everything you need to escape. Open The King's Compass, tune into His voice, and stay on The Way Road. The Dragon wants to keep you asleep, but your Father calls you to wake up and walk boldly toward Him.

Your light is needed here. Shine brightly, Princess, and show the world what it means to belong to The King.

Watch Out! It's A Trap!

So, here's the thing about the enemy—he's not creative. Just consistent. He's been using the same three traps since the beginning of time: lust, pride, and the eyes. And honestly? We keep falling for them like it's the first time. Let's expose the bait and choose better.

> *Let's break it down, shall we?*

Lust of The Flesh

This is a fleshly desire that comes from that part of you that has been poisoned and brainwashed to rebel against your Father's Kingdom. Simply put, it is pleasure-seeking behavior that works to draw you away from your Father's presence.

This poisoned passion causes you to desire things that are bad for you. Things like drugs, greed, and sexual immorality are just some of the sins that come with this trap. Speaking of sexual immorality, it is important to note that sexual sin is a huge part of this one. That means watching something that is sexually stimulating is sin. That means that sex outside of marriage is sin. Period.

Once you let your flesh rule, it will run you into destruction. Do not feed your flesh. Avoid this trap at all cost!

Scripture Anchor:
"For if you live according to the flesh you will die, but if by the Spirit you put to death the deeds of the body, you will live." (Romans 8:13)

Lust of the Eyes

Simply put, the lust of the eyes is the desire to possess what we see or to engage in those things that visually appeal to our fleshly appetite. So basically, this is anything you put in front of your eyes that will cause you to sin.

The most obvious examples of this would be things that you literally watch that are sinful—things like inappropriate TV, movies, websites, games, magazines, etc. What you look at has the power to stumble you.

Another way this trap works is through jealousy and covetousness. To see someone else's belongings and want their things for yourself is wrong.

As a girl in Dystopia, you will encounter many thought bombs. The best way to avoid them is to stay clear of them.

Scripture Anchor:
"For everything in the world—the lust of the flesh, the lust of the eyes, and the pride of life—comes not from the Father but from the world." (1 John 2:16)

Pride of of Life

The Bible tells us that "Pride comes before a fall." Pride is the original sin that caused you to fall away from your Father in the first place. It doesn't matter its size—ALL PRIDE IS BAD. Even the smallest form of pride will seek to grow and take over your life. It starts with a single thought.

For example, you might think to yourself, "I am the smartest girl in my class." If left unchecked, that thought will grow to, "I am better than everyone in my class." And eventually, that thought can lead you to disrespect, despise, and even hurt your classmates because of your prideful heart.

Pride leads to all sin. So guard your heart at all cost against this one.

Scripture Anchor:
"Pride goes before destruction, a haughty spirit before a fall." (Proverbs 16:18)

Points to Ponder

- Am I chasing things that feel good but pull me away from God?

- What am I watching or scrolling through that might be hurting my heart or my mind?

- Do I ever catch myself comparing my life to someone else's and feeling jealous or less-than?

- Have I let pride sneak in through compliments, achievements, or "just being right"?

- Is there anything I've been ignoring that I know deep down my Father wants me to walk away from?

Let's Bring It In

The enemy's traps—lust, pride, and the eyes—are sneaky, targeted, and always dressed to distract. But you're not defenseless.
Your Father gave you tools:
- Prayer to stay connected.
- The Sword to cut through the lies.
- Faith to keep walking even when it's dark.

You weren't meant to wander lost in Dystopia. You were meant to fight smart, walk strong, and live free.
So stay alert, open your toolbox, and use what your Father gave you.
Because the enemy may be loud—but he's already lost.

4
Heavenly Help

Now that you know who's against you, let Me show you who's for you.

You've got the strongest team in existence—Team Heaven. God the Father rules with love and power. Jesus—your White Knight—already won the battle. And I walk with you every step of the way. And did I mention you have angels protecting and fighting for you too? Yup, they're real, they're fierce, and they've got orders to protect you. With so many heavenly beings on your side, you are never alone.

One God, Three Persons
What's Up With The Trinity?

Before we jump into the next section, let's clear something up— because you're about to hear about the Father, the Savior, and the Holy Spirit (The Helper) ... and yes, all three are God.

Confusing? I get it.

Here's the truth:
The Father, the Son and the Spirit are One God in Three Persons—not three different gods, not three masks, not one God switching outfits. We are always united. Always in sync. Always love.

The Father is The King—eternal, holy, and full of wisdom.
The Son is Jesus—your Savior, the White Knight who walked The Way Road and gave His life to save you.

The Helper (That's Me) is God's Spirit who lives inside you, guiding, comforting, and cheering you on.

Still confused? Well let's try to break it down a little more.

Let's use an earthly example to help us understand.

Imagine an orange. You've got:

- The peel – It covers. It's not the whole fruit, but you can't get to the inside without it. That's kind of like the Father—majestic, powerful, holding all things together.

- The juicy fruit – Sweet, nourishing, bursting with flavor. That's like the Son, Jesus—the part of God you can taste, touch, and see. He walked among you and gave His life so you could live.

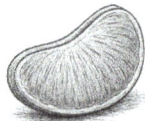

- The seed inside – Small, often hidden, but packed with life. That's God's Spirit—The Helper. He plants truth inside your heart, helps things grow, and keeps you connected to the Source.

One orange. Three parts. Same fruit.
Each part has its own role, but you can't separate them without losing the full picture.

Hopefully that helps a bit. Truthfully, you may still be a little confused —and that's okay. If you could figure out the entire nature of God and box it up with a bow... well, that wouldn't be much of a God, would it? So yes, it should still feel a little mysterious.

But here's the part you *can* understand:
God loves you. God is with you.
And all three of Us are working together to bring you safely home.

OUR FATHER IN HEAVEN

Let me tell you about Him. Not just The King. Not just the Maker. The Beginning and the End. The One who lit the stars with His voice and hung galaxies like chandeliers.

He is holy—meaning set apart. He is perfect, above and beyond comprehension. He is justice—never wrong, never unfair, never late. He is love—he's not just loving... He is Love itself.

And somehow... Miraculously... He is *also* your Father.

Let's Break It Down

The Eternal King Who Became Your Dad

Before there was time, there was Him. Before there were angels, atoms, or any concept of "you," He was already planning your story. Not just the shell of your life, but every detail: your laugh, your tears, your quirks, your calling.

He made you in His image, not because He needed anything—but because love always gives. And He did. He placed eternity in your heart and His love in your soul. And then, when sin tried to steal you—He didn't flinch. He sent Jesus, His only Son, not as a backup plan, but as the Master plan.

The Father's wrath against sin is real. But so is His mercy. The cross wasn't a reaction. It was a rescue mission. And it came straight from the Father's heart. Now that's love!

Scripture Anchor:
"You saw me before I was born. Every day of my life was recorded in your book. Every moment was laid out before a single day had passed." (Psalm 139:16)

The Father's Plan for Your Life

Let's talk about *the plan*—because yes, there is one.
You may not see it clearly. Some days, it might feel like all you've got are pieces: broken dreams, painful memories, unanswered prayers. But your Father sees the whole picture. He's not making it up as He goes. He's not surprised by the mess or thrown off by your pain. He's a master builder—and nothing gets wasted.

That heartbreak? He'll use it. That detour you hated? It's already rerouted for your good. Even the dark chapters— the trauma, the tears, the things no one else knows—He's already weaving them into a story that ends in victory. He doesn't always explain every moment, but He promises that every moment is part of something bigger, something good. And here's the cherry on top: Princess, your Father is perfect. Not sorta-good. Not mostly-wise. But PERFECT! And you? You're precious to Him.

So even when it doesn't make sense, even when the road is rough, you can trust this: He knows exactly what He's doing with your life, and He's doing it with love.

Scripture Anchor:
"For I know the plans I have for you,' declares the Lord, 'plans to prosper you and not to harm you, plans to give you a hope and a future." — Jeremiah 29:11

Points to Ponder

- What would change in your life if you really believed that the Creator of the universe calls you His daughter?

- Have you been resenting the pain in your story instead of trusting God to redeem it?

- If He's perfect and you are precious... isn't He worthy of your full trust?

Let's Bring It In

The Father is not distant, silent, or cold. He's the One who named you, claimed you, and calls you His own. His voice speaks louder than shame, deeper than doubt or any lie the enemy whispers.

And His plan? It's not random or careless. It weaves every tear, every twist, every triumph into something beautiful. Even the hardest chapters can be redeemed in His hands. So take heart, Princess. You're not just seen—you're being shaped by a perfect Father who loves you more than you can imagine. And He's not done with your story yet.

Jesus: The White Knight

Let's set the scene, Princess.

You're not just stuck, you're trapped. Not *forgot-your-password* trapped. No. This is *dragon-guarded enchanted-tower in a forest-full-of-lies* kind of trapped. And every glitter-wrapped lie keeps whispering that no one is coming to get you.

But that's not true. Because your Father saw you there, and He couldn't stand to leave you that way.
So, He sent Jesus. Not as backup. Not as a last resort.
He sent His very best. His only Son. Your White Knight.

But All Is Not Lost!!!

Enter Jesus—The White Knight

Just when the shadows feel too thick to escape—boom. The ground shakes. The walls crack. Light crashes through like Heaven itself just kicked in the gate.
And Jesus steps onto the scene.

Not just a Savior. Not just a King. But your White Knight.
He doesn't sneak in quietly—He rides in fierce. His armor glows with holy light. His eyes burn with love and fire. And His sword? It's not for show—it's the Sword of Truth. One swing, and the chains snap like threads. The lies vanish like shadows when the sun breaks through.

The Dragon tries to roar—but it's too late. The war was already won.

Jesus defeated the enemy the moment He gave His life for you. And when He rose from the grave three days later? That sealed it. The keys to death, fear, shame, and every trap that ever held you? Yeah—He's holding them now.
You are rescued. Fully. Finally. Forever.

Scripture Anchor:
"For God so loved the world, that he gave his only begotten Son, that whosoever believe in him should not perish, but have everlasting life." (John 3:16)

The Savior Who Stays

Here's the wild part: Jesus doesn't just show up, save you, and leave. He stays. He lifts you up, carries you out of the mess—and then He walks beside you, step by step.

He's not just there in the big dragon-slaying moments, but in the quiet ones too. He's with you at the lonely lunch tables, for the ugly cries and for the crazy thoughts that cycle in your mind at 2AM.

He's there for it all.
He didn't *just* rescue you from eternal destruction.
He's keeps you in the everyday stuff too.

And why? Not because you impressed Him. Not because you earned Him. But because He looked at you, trapped and trembling, and said: "She's mine. I'll do whatever it takes to bring her back."

And He did.

Scripture Anchor:
"For it is by grace you have been saved, through faith—and this is not from yourselves, it is the gift of God."
(Ephesians 2:8)

Scripture Anchor:
"But God showed his great love for us by sending Christ to die for us while we were still sinners." (Romans 5:8)

Points to Ponder

- Now ask yourself, Princess: With a love this full, this faithful, this forever...how much of your life does He deserve in return?

- Jesus broke every chain, so why would we put ourselves back in bondage to sin if He freed us?

- What does a life totally surrendered to Jesus look like—and are you living that life?

Let's Bring It In

The Father sent His only Son, Jesus, to break every chain and silence every lie that tried to keep you from Him. Jesus didn't just rescue you —He rides beside you, walks with you, and leads you home.

He is the Knight who never leaves. The Savior who already won... because He conquered death and the grave just to rescue you.
And He's not going anywhere.

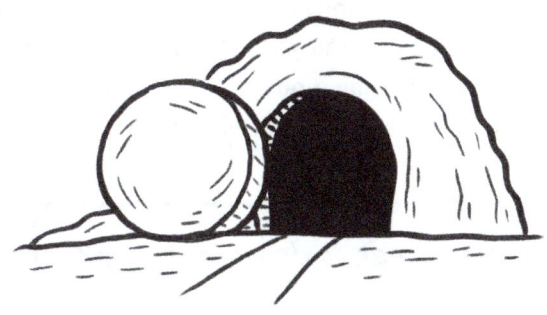

Who Is The Helper?

Hey there, Princess. It may seem like we just met—but I've known you forever. Before you ever picked up this book, before your first breath, before your heart ever wondered if you were truly seen... I was there. Sent by The King Himself.

I am The Helper. You might know Me by another name—The Holy Spirit. But don't let that title make Me feel far away or hard to reach. I'm not floating somewhere above your life. I'm walking beside you. Living inside you.

I'm here because The King couldn't bear to leave you alone in the dark. So He made a way—a costly, beautiful, forever kind of way. He sent the closest part of His heart. He sent The White Knight, Jesus.

It happened on a hill.
Jesus rode into battle and gave everything He had. He took your place. He broke the curse. He tore the veil. And when He rose from the grave, He made it possible for Me to come dwell with you—forever.

I was sent because Jesus finished what you never could.
So here I am. I've been calling you, drawing you to the truth your entire life. And once you opened your eyes to the light... I entered your heart to walk with you from the inside.

Let's break it down, shall we?

I'm Your Best Friend

You know that one friend who always knows what to say, shows up exactly when you need them, and never, ever lets you down?

You're probably saying, "No one is that perfect. That kind of friend doesn't exist." And you'd be right—if we were just talking about humans. But I'm no human. I am the very Spirit of The King: perfectly everywhere, conveniently all-knowing, and fueled with the power of your Father.

And guess what? I'm totally committed to you.
That's me. I'm here for all of it—the victories, the mess-ups, the tears, and the laughter. Feeling overwhelmed? I'm here. Not sure which way to turn? I'll guide you. Need someone to celebrate with? I'm your biggest fan. You're never alone because I'm always by your side.

And like any good best friend, I bring gifts. Not just birthday-style blessings or glittery surprises (though I do love to celebrate), but I give the kind of gifts that change you from the inside out: peace that can't be stolen, joy that doesn't depend on circumstance, wisdom beyond your years, boldness when you're scared, and love that never runs out. I can even empower you to do the miraculous. I know just the right gift to give you at just the right time. And the gifts I give are way more precious than riches and gold.

But here's something else you need to know: I'm not a robot. I'm not cold, distant, or disconnected. I'm real. I feel.

So when you walk off The Way Road—the path that leads home to your Father's kingdom—it grieves Me. Not because I'm mad at you, but because I love you. I see the traps. I know where those side trails lead. And when you ignore My voice or shut Me out, My heart aches.

I'm not here to guilt-trip you. I'm here to guide you. To restore you. To cheer you on. I'll keep whispering truth, leading you, comforting you... keeping you.

Because I'm your BFF.

So lean in. Talk to Me. Trust Me. Let Me be the friend who never leaves, never lies, and never fails. Because that's exactly who I am.

Scripture Anchor:
"Then I will ask My Father and He will give you another Helper. He will be with you forever. He is the Spirit of Truth. The world cannot receive Him. It does not see Him or know Him. You know Him because He lives with you and will be in you." (John 14:16-17)

I'm Your Guide, Comfort, and Helper

Life's a maze, isn't it? So many voices. So many choices. But don't panic—I know the way. I'll nudge you left when danger's right. I'll drop peace in your heart when you're about to step into something that'll hurt. I speak through Scripture, through wise people, and sometimes through a deep, quiet knowing you can't explain.

When life feels too heavy, I'll carry what you can't. When the sadness sneaks in, I'll wrap you in The King's love until it lifts. You were never meant to do this on your own. That's why I'm here.

And when the battle feels too big? I'll be your strength. You don't need to fake it or "try harder." Just lean into Me, and I'll give you what you need in the moment. I always show up. Every time. Always.

Scripture Anchor:
"May the God of hope fill you with all joy and peace as you trust in him, so that you may overflow with hope by the power of The Holy Spirit." (Romans 15:13)

I'm The King's Voice

When The King speaks, I'm the one who delivers His message straight to your heart. And when The Dragon tries to fill your head with lies, I'll be the louder voice, declaring The King's truth over you.

I was sent by your heavenly Father—not as an idea or a feeling, but as His breath, His whisper, His voice. When you hear Me, you are hearing Him. I speak what I hear from the throne and carry it straight to your heart.

You've felt Me before—in the quiet pull to pray, in the weight of conviction wrapped in mercy, in that strange peace that doesn't make sense. That was Me. And when The Dragon and the world of Dystopia tried to drown you out with lies and noise, I was the still, small voice saying, "Come back."

I am the voice of the Savior, too. I remind you of what He said. I anchor you in what He finished. When you forget who you are, I remind you who He is. When your knees shake under guilt, I hold out grace. When you're too tired to speak, I intercede with groanings deeper than words.

You don't have to beg Me to show up—I already have. So listen. Not with your ears, but with your heart.
The King is speaking. And I am His voice.

Scripture Anchor:
"And he who searches our hearts knows the mind of the Spirit, because the Spirit intercedes for God's people in accordance with the will of God." (Romans 8:27)

Points to Ponder

- When the world is loud and confusing, do I stop and listen for The Holy Spirit's voice of truth?

- Am I letting The Holy Spirit guide my choices—or just asking Him to bless the ones I already made?

- Do I treat Him like the friend He truly is, or do I keep Him at a distance until things go wrong?

Let's Bring It In

So you've learned that I'm your guide, your comforter, your helper (yup, that's my name), and I'm your Father's voice. And you may be thinking, "With a friend like this, I'm all set! Nothing can stop me." But that's not entirely accurate. Here's the thing: I'm always with you, but staying close takes effort.

Talk to Me. Invite Me into your decisions, your challenges, and your celebrations. I want to hear it all—the big stuff, the small stuff, and everything in between. And when you're not sure if it's Me or your own thoughts, compare what you hear to The King's Compass (the Word of God). I'll never contradict Him.

Princess, I was sent to make sure you never have to walk this journey alone. I'm your constant reminder of how deeply The King loves you. Lean on Me, trust Me, and let Me help you shine brighter than ever. Together, we'll make it back to The Kingdom—and have some incredible adventures along the way.

What About Angels?

You've probably seen the cheesy cartoons—angels floating on clouds, strumming harps, glowing softly like spiritual nightlights. Cute, but way off. The real deal? They're warriors. Messengers. Guardians. Think more elite special forces than sparkly sky babies. And here's the wild part: they're on your side (well, the good ones are, anyway).

But before we go further, a quick but important disclaimer: angels are powerful, yes—but they are not God. They aren't to be worshipped, prayed to, or idolized. Real angels would be the first to say that. In fact, in Revelation 22:9, when John tried to bow to an angel, the angel said, "Don't do that! I am a fellow servant with you... Worship God!"

Angels serve The King. They take orders from your Father. They may look glorious, but they're your fellow soldiers in The Kingdom—sent to help, not be honored. They fight for you because He commands them to.

> *Let's break it down, shall we?*

Protection Sent By The Father

Let's rewind to the Bible for a moment. Remember Elisha and his servant in 2 Kings 6? They were surrounded by an enemy army—completely outnumbered.

The servant freaked out (as one does), but Elisha calmly prayed, "Lord, open his eyes." Suddenly, the servant saw it: the hills were full of horses and chariots of fire—angel armies ready for battle.

Well… That's not just a one-time miracle. It's still happening. You might not see flaming chariots outside your window (which, honestly, would be awesome), but that doesn't mean they're not there.

Angels are constantly at work—fighting spiritual battles you can't see, keeping you safe on highways, walking with you into schools, homes, hospitals, and hard conversations. Every divine rescue, close call, or unexplained protection? You can thank The King—and His warriors.

Scripture Anchor:
"For he will command his angels concerning you to guard you in all your ways." (Psalm 91:11)

Encouragers and Guides in Disguise

Angels don't just fight—they show up when you need direction or hope, too.

Ever felt a sudden nudge to take a different route, say something kind to a stranger, or show up somewhere you almost skipped—and it turned out to matter more than you knew? Maybe you were being rerouted for a divine appointment. Maybe an angel was involved.

In Scripture, angels often showed up with exactly what was needed. They told Mary about Jesus. They encouraged Gideon when he felt worthless. They strengthened Jesus Himself in the Garden when He was in agony.

And they still move today.

That encouragement that shows up right before you're about to break? That moment you feel peace out of nowhere in the middle of chaos? Maybe it's not "out of nowhere." Maybe heaven is closer than you think.

Scripture Anchor:
"Don't forget to show hospitality to strangers, for some who have done this have entertained angels without realizing it!" (Hebrews 13:2)

Points to Ponder

- Have you ever experienced a moment of unexpected protection or encouragement that might've been divine intervention?

- If angels obey God without hesitation, what does that say about the way we should respond to His voice?

- If angels rejoice over one sinner who repents, what do you think heaven sounded like the day you said yes to Jesus?

- What if that delay, detour, or closed door was actually divine redirection through angelic protection?

Let's Bring It In

You're never as alone as you feel. The King of Heaven doesn't just send comfort—He sends company. Warrior angels surround you. Messenger angels guide you. Comforting angels support you. You walk through life surrounded by heavenly help, even when you can't see it.

So don't forget, Princess: you have more backup than you know.

5
Godly Character

Your character may be the only evidence someone will ever see that your Father is real.

The way you speak, the way you treat others, the way you live when no one's watching... it all points to something. Or Someone.

Because you are an ambassador for your Father's Kingdom. That means you don't just represent yourself—you represent Him. And while crowns are lovely, it's your character that truly shows the world who your Dad is. But don't worry—I'm not asking you to fake it or force it. That's not how The Kingdom works. The Father and the Savior have asked Me to grow it in you, one step at a time.

The Fruit of the Spirit

Hey Princess.

Let's take a second before we begin. Breathe in slow. Now exhale. You've been holding in a lot—a lot of questions, feelings, hurts and offenses. Like that thing someone said that still kinda stings. You've been trying so hard to be good. To be kind. To be "spiritual."

And maybe you're wondering...
"If I'm really walking with God, why do I still lose my temper? Why do I still mess up? Why does patience feel like a fairy tale?"

Let Me tell you something right here, right now: you are growing. Even when it doesn't feel like it. Even when you feel more mess than masterpiece. You are Mine. And I'm growing something holy in you called the Fruit of the Spirit. Not bananas and berries. No. I'm talking about spiritual fruit.

This fruit is proof—solid hard proof—that you belong to Me. So, Princess, let's walk through your garden together and see what's blooming.

61

The Peopling Fruits

These fruits show up when you're doing life with other people—yes, even the difficult ones These are the fruits I grow in you when your friends are moody, your family's too loud, and the adults in your life just don't understand.

Kindness

Kindness—this is caring in motion. the moment you carry someone's books, send that "you okay?" text, or let the kid who never gets picked join your game. Kindness doesn't need a stage—it just needs a heart that sees. And when kindness grows bolder, it becomes Goodness.

 ### Scripture Anchor:
"Be kind and compassionate to one another, forgiving each other, just as in Christ God forgave you." (Ephesians 4:32)

Goodness

Goodness is choosing what's right when no one's watching. It's turning down the gossip and choosing grace instead. It's standing up for someone when no one else sees. When there's no audience but Me.

And if I see—your Father sees too. And Princess, that's all that matters.

Patience

Patience—the silent superhero of this group. Patience is waiting with grace. It's listening without interrupting. It's choosing not to scream when things move slower than you want them to. It's holding your words when snapping would feel better.

Patience whispers, "God's not in a hurry. So I don't need to be either." And when you hear that whisper and choose to trust it? That's fruit. Real, growing, heaven-planted fruit.

The Inward, Quiet Fruits

These are the inward fruits, the ones you feel deeply. They grow in the quiet corners of your heart, where your thoughts swirl and your emotions stretch.

Joy

Joy shows up in the weirdest places. Like in the middle of a messy cry that somehow turns into laughter. In the quiet moment after disappointment, when your heart still manages to whisper, "God is good." Because even if things don't work out the way you hoped... you're still His. Jesus still died for you. He still rose again. And your Father still loves you—and He's doing everything to get you back home.

This is why your joy can't be stolen. Because it's not based in this world of Dystopia. Your joy comes from your Father's Kingdom. It holds you steady—not because life is easy, but because you know who holds your life.

 *Scripture Anchor:*
"In Your presence (Lord) is fullness of joy; at Your right hand are pleasures forevermore." (Psalm 16:11)

Peace

Peace is like joy—it doesn't depend on anything in this world. Not your friends, not your home life, not your social media chats. None of that. Peace is Me breathing into your spirit, reminding you that We—Me, your Father, and your Savior—We got you. The storm may be raging and the waves might be high... but you're not in the boat alone. I'm right there with you. And I promise, I'll get you to the other side.

Scripture Anchor:

Do not be anxious about anything, but in every situation, by prayer and petition, with thanksgiving, present your requests to God. And the peace of God, which transcends all understanding, will guard your hearts and your minds in Christ Jesus. (Philippians 4:6-7)

Self Control

It's what helps you shut your mouth when you're ready to snap back. It's what keeps you from the thing you *can* do but probably shouldn't. It's the quiet, holy pause that says, "Nope, I want a better outcome than this." Self-control is Me working into you the poise of heaven. With it, there's no obstacle you won't be able to overcome.

Scripture Anchor:

"A person without self-control is like a city with broken-down walls." (Proverbs 25:28)

The Level-Up Fruits

These fruits show up when you're growing stronger. When your roots are getting deeper. This is where you step into who you really are, Princess. These are the royal fruits.

Faithfulness

Faithfulness is what steadies you. It's the quiet "yes" you say to God when the glory of the mountaintop is gone. It's reading your Bible when it doesn't feel exciting. It's praying even when heaven feels quiet. Staying loyal when no one's cheering you on. Being a friend when it costs you something. Choosing God again and again—even when it would be easier not to. Faithfulness isn't loud, but oh is it powerful! It doesn't quit when it gets boring. It keeps going because it knows Who it's walking with. And that makes all the difference.

Scripture Anchor:
Let love and faithfulness never leave you; bind them around your neck, write them on the tablet of your heart. Then you will win favor and a good name in the sight of God and man. (Proverbs 3:3-4)

Gentleness

This is strength in soft wrapping. It's power with polish. It's how royalty moves. It's when you could yell, but you don't. When you could tear someone down, but you decide to speak life instead. Gentleness doesn't mean letting people walk over you. It means walking in confidence, with grace in your hands and wisdom on your tongue. It's how Jesus spoke to the hurting—truthful, but never cruel. Strong, but never harsh. It's the heart of the Father being woven in you.

Scripture Anchor:
"Let your gentleness be evident to all. The Lord is near." (Philippians 4:5)

All of this fruit is held in the basket of... Love.

Love is what ties it all together. It's not just one fruit on the list—if the fruit are the patches, then love is the quilt that holds them together. Without love, patience turns bitter. Kindness becomes performance. Goodness grows rigid. Joy runs shallow. Peace won't last. Faithfulness falters. Gentleness fades. And self-control? It snaps.

But when love is present—real, deep, God-rooted love—everything else grows the way it was meant to.
Love is the seed I planted in you the moment Jesus, your Knight in shining armor, saved you. When I entered your heart, I promised to keep you through this world, guide you home, and grow you along the way. Love was the seed. And the fruit? Let's just say you're tending your own Eden in that heart of yours.

I'm proud of you, Princess. I really am.

Points to Ponder

- Which fruit do I see growing in my life right now?

- Which one feels the hardest to live out and why?

- Who in my life needs a taste of the fruit God's growing in me?

Taming the Terrible Tongue

Picture this: your tongue is a loose cannon—literally. It's perched on a wobbly pirate ship in the middle of your life, wildly firing shots left and right. BOOM! There goes a friendship. CRASH! That's a rumor ricocheting back at you. And just when you think it's under control, it fires again, taking out the peace at lunch or sinking a perfectly fine group chat.

The tongue is small, but its power is colossal. It can steer your relationships toward unity or chaos with just a few words. Gossip, in particular, is like loading the cannon with explosive ammo. It promises excitement and connection but leaves behind charred bridges and scorched trust. The King calls you to tame the terrible tongue—not just for the sake of others, but for the peace and light it brings to your own heart.

Let's break it down, shall we?

The Spark of Gossip: Why It's So Tempting

The cannon of gossip often goes off when you least expect it. You're just hanging out, talking about nothing, and suddenly, someone says, "Did you hear about...?" That's when the temptation hits. It feels like slipping a cannonball of juicy details into the barrel and lighting the fuse. Sharing it makes you feel included, funny, or even admired for knowing the inside scoop.

But here's the reality: gossip doesn't connect people—it causes collateral damage. Someone's reputation gets blasted, trust shatters, and even your own credibility takes a hit. Proverbs warns us: "The tongue has the power of life and death" (Proverbs 18:21). When you gossip, you're not just firing shots at someone else—you're sabotaging your own character.

Before you speak, ask yourself, "Am I loading my cannon with life or destruction?" Every word you choose has the potential to either build up or blow apart the lives of those around you.

Scripture Anchor:
"Those who guard their mouths and their tongues keep themselves from calamity." (Proverbs 21:23)

The Damage is Done

The tongue is small, but it's dangerous. Once words fly out, you can't grab them back. They cut through hearts like darts —fast, sharp, and impossible to reverse. A mean joke, a careless insult, or a whispered rumor might feel small in the moment, but once spoken, it lands deep.

You can say "I didn't mean it" or "I'm sorry," and that helps— but the sting still lingers. Words carry power. They can build up or they can tear down. That's why God calls us to guard our tongues and choose words that bring life, not destruction.

Next time you feel ready to launch those darts, pause and ask yourself, "Will this heal or will this harm?" Once the dart is thrown, the damage is done. But when we use our tongues with care, they can be tools of kindness, encouragement, and peace.

Scripture Anchor:
"A troublemaker plants seeds of strife; gossip separates the best of friends" (Proverbs 16:28)

The King's Call to Love

Your cannon is only as powerful as the ammo you put inside it. So ask yourself... what am I loading my cannon with? Are you loading it with truth, kindness, and encouragement? Or are you packing it with judgment, negativity, and half-truths? The wrong ammunition will always backfire, leaving a trail of hurt that's hard to repair.

Think about the last time you gossiped. Were you sharing something true or just something sensational? Were you speaking to build someone up or to tear them down? Maybe you were venting frustration or jealousy—those emotional cannonballs hit just as hard. The King calls us to use our words as tools for peace, not destruction.

Love is the ammunition The King wants you to load. It doesn't just mean avoiding gossip—it means actively choosing to speak life into every situation. When someone shares a struggle, love encourages instead of criticizes. It stops the rumor instead of passing it on. Love means using your words to reflect The King's heart.

When you choose to speak with love, your cannon becomes a tool for light instead of destruction. Your words inspire hope, repair broken trust, and show others what it means to be a daughter of The King.

Scripture Anchor:
"Do not let any unwholesome talk come out of your mouths, but only what is helpful for building others up according to their needs, that it may benefit those who listen."
(Ephesians 4:29)

Points to Ponder

- What lights the fuse of gossip for you? Think about what situations or emotions—like boredom, frustration, or the desire to feel included—tempt you to gossip, and consider how you can redirect those impulses.

- How would it feel to be in the blast zone? Reflect on times you've been hurt by gossip. Ask yourself: "If these words were about me, how would I feel?"

- What are you loading your cannon with? Evaluate whether your words build others up with kindness and grace or spread harm through judgment and negativity.

- Have you fired shots recently? Think about any relationships that might have been strained by gossip and how you can take steps to rebuild trust and offer peace.

Let's Bring It In

Let's sum it up.
Check your motives and moments—what triggers your urge to gossip? Whether it's boredom, insecurity, or the need to belong, recognize the fuse before it's lit. Put yourself in the blast zone—would you want those words said about you? Examine your verbal ammo: are your words loaded with grace and truth or judgment and harm? And if you've fired shots, it's not too late to rebuild trust. Own it, apologize, and choose love moving forward. You got this Princess.

A Girl of Integrity

Hey there, Princess! Let's talk about one of the most underrated yet most dazzling accessories a royal daughter can wear: integrity. It's not a tiara or a sparkling gown (though those are fun too). No, integrity is your badge of honor—a gleaming symbol of who you are when no one else is looking. In The Kingdom of Lights, integrity isn't just a good idea; it's essential for every princess walking The Way Road.

But what is integrity, really? It's living in truth, staying honest, and doing the right thing even when it's hard. It's choosing the high road (yes, even when The Dragon tempts you to take the shortcut). Integrity isn't just something you do; it's who you are.

Let's break it down, shall we?

Integrity is About Wholeness

The word "integrity" comes from the idea of being whole, complete, and undivided. It's about being the same person in private as you are in public. No masks. No pretending. Just you, walking in the light of truth.

When you live with integrity, you're not trying to impress anyone or hide behind a facade. You're standing confidently as the princess The King created you to be. And let's be honest: there's nothing more freeing than living a life where you don't have to remember the lies you told or the corners you cut.

 *Scripture Anchor:*
"Whoever walks in integrity walks securely, but he who makes his ways crooked will be found out." (Proverbs 10:9)

Integrity Builds Trust

Every relationship—with friends, family, and even The King Himself—needs trust. And trust? It's built on integrity. When people know that your words match your actions, they see you as dependable, loyal, and true. You become a light in a world full of shadows.

And here's the kicker: when you live with integrity, people will notice. They'll see something different about you, something real. They might not understand it at first, but they'll be drawn to it. Why? Because integrity reflects The King's character. It's like wearing His badge of honor for everyone to see.

 *Scripture Anchor:*
"Whoever can be trusted with very little can also be trusted with much, and whoever is dishonest with very little will also be dishonest with much." (Luke 16:10)

Points to Ponder

- Be Honest: Always tell the truth, even when it's hard. Lies might seem easier in the moment, but they're cracks in your foundation.

- Keep Your Promises: If you say you'll do something, follow through. Your word is golden, Princess.

- Do the Right Thing: Even when no one is watching, choose what's right over what's easy.

- Own Your Mistakes: Nobody's perfect, and that's okay. When you mess up, admit it, ask for forgiveness, and make it right.

- Seek The King's Guidance: Pray for wisdom and strength to walk in integrity every day.

Let's Bring It In

The King values integrity because it reflects His heart. He is truth, and as His daughter, you're called to live in that truth. When you walk in integrity, you're not just honoring Him—you're becoming more like Him. And that, Princess, is the greatest honor of all.

So wear your badge of integrity proudly. Let it shine brighter than your jewels and speak louder than your words. The King sees you, He's proud of you, and He's walking with you every step of The Way Road.

6
People in My Life

People can be… a lot. A lot of good or a lot of everything else.

Some pour sunshine into your soul. Others roll in like thunderstorms. And a few manage to be both—your biggest cheer squad one day, your patience-tester the next.

Here's the secret: your Father uses every single one of them. None of them are accidents. The difficult ones are divine assignments. The delightful ones are sharpening tools.

So let's slow down and meet the cast—discover who they are, how they shape you, and how The King might be weaving each encounter into something beautiful.

Moms: The Royal Advisors of Your Story

Whether she's your biggest cheerleader or your toughest critic (or a complicated mix of both), your mom has a unique role in your royal adventure. She's not just another character in your story; she's someone who's walked the very path you're on now. And that makes her one of The King's best tools for guiding you home.

But before we dive in, let's get real: not every mom fits the fairy tale. Some moms struggle. Some moms hurt. And some moms… well, let's just say their crowns feel a little crooked. Whatever your situation, remember this: The King sees it all, and He's working it together for your good.

> Let's break it down, shall we?

The Wisdom of a Mom Who's Been There

Your mom might feel like she's from another universe sometimes (and honestly, with some of her outdated slang, maybe she is). But here's the deal: she's been where you are. She's faced the dragons of peer pressure, scaled the towers of self-doubt, and probably made a few wrong turns on The Way Road herself. And because of that, she has wisdom you can't find in a book or a YouTube video.

Think of her as your royal advisor—not perfect, but appointed by The King to help you navigate life. When she gives advice, it's not to ruin your fun or keep you from living your best life. It's because she's seen the pitfalls and wants to spare you the pain. Sure, it might feel annoying at times (cue the eye rolls), but don't underestimate the gift of her experience.

Scripture Anchor:
"She opens her mouth with wisdom, and the teaching of kindness is on her tongue." (Proverbs 31:26)

What About Crooked Crowns?

Now, let's talk about the tough stuff. Not all moms wear their crowns with grace. Some carry scars, struggles, and stories that make it hard for them to love the way they'd like to. If your mom's crown feels a little crooked, remember this: her imperfections don't define your story. The King's love and guidance can fill in the gaps where human love falls short.

Maybe your mom is distant, critical, or maybe she's just not there. That hurts. But here's the royal truth: The King can use even the hardest parts of your story to shape you into the princess He's called you to be. He's the ultimate parent, and His love is steady, unchanging, and perfect. When your earthly mom stumbles, lean into Him.

Scripture Anchor:
"Can a mother forget the baby at her breast and have no compassion on the child she has borne? Though she may forget, I will not forget you!" (Isaiah 49:15)

When Listening Feels Impossible

Let's be real: sometimes it feels like your mom just doesn't get it. Maybe her rules feel outdated, her advice feels irrelevant, or her tone gets on your last nerve. But here's a royal challenge for you: listen anyway. Why? Because honor isn't about agreeing with everything she says, it's about respecting the role The King gave her in your life.

When you listen—really listen—you're not just obeying your mom; you're honoring The King. And that kind of obedience brings blessings beyond what you can see right now.

Scripture Anchor:
"Listen, my son, to your father's instruction and do not forsake your mother's teaching." (Proverbs 1:8)

Points to Ponder

- **Pray for Her:** Whether your mom is a saint or a struggler, she needs prayer. Ask The King to give her strength, wisdom, and grace for her role as your mom.

- **Speak Life:** Words are powerful. Choose ones that uplift and encourage, even when you feel frustrated. A kind word can soften even the hardest hearts.

- **Be Patient:** Moms are human. They make mistakes, have bad days, and sometimes let their emotions get the best of them. Give her grace, just as The King gives it to you.

- **Say Thank You:** A simple "thank you" can go a long way. Acknowledge the sacrifices she makes, big or small, and let her know you appreciate her.

- **Lean on The King:** When your relationship with your mom feels strained, remember that The King is your ultimate source of love, guidance, and comfort.

Let's Bring It In

Princess, your mom isn't perfect, but she's part of your royal story for a reason. Whether she's your best friend, your biggest challenge, or somewhere in between, The King placed her in your life to help shape you into the person He's calling you to be. Listen to her wisdom, love her through her flaws, and trust The King to work all things—even the hard moments—together for your good.

Dads: The King's Provider and Protector

Dads are a gift from The King, sent to provide, protect, and guide you as you walk The Way Road. But let's be real—sometimes it's not all fairytales and father-daughter dances. Relationships with Dads can be as complex as the stories in the royal library. So let's dive into what makes Dad's role so important and how The King uses him in your journey.

> *Let's break it down, shall we?*

What Dads Do

First and foremost, Dad is a provider. He's the one who works hard to make sure there's food on the table, a roof over your head, and, if he's extra awesome, some surprise chocolate chip cookies in the pantry. But more than that, Dad provides wisdom, advice, and a steady hand when life gets shaky.

He's also your protector. Whether he's scaring away imaginary monsters under the bed or giving that *you'd-better-be-respectful* look to anyone who's not treating you like the princess you are, Dad's mission is to keep you safe. He's been given this role by The King, who Himself is the ultimate Provider and Protector.

Scripture Anchor:
"Hear, O sons (and daughters), a father's instruction, and be attentive, that you may gain insight." (Proverbs 4:1)

81

When Dad Gets It Right

Let's celebrate the times when Dad nails it. Maybe he's the dad who prays with you every night, who shows up to every recital or game, and who always knows how to make you laugh. Those moments are glimpses of The King's heart, Princess. Your Dad, as flawed as he may be, is reflecting the love of the ultimate Father.

 *Scripture Anchor:*
"Honor your father and your mother, that your days may be long in the land that the Lord your God is giving you." (Exodus 20:12)

When Dad Falls Short

Here's the hard truth: not all dads live up to their role. Some are absent, some are unkind, and some struggle to show the love and care The King intended. If your relationship with your dad feels more like a stormy sea than a safe harbor, know this: The King sees you. He knows your pain, and He promises to use even this part of your story for good.

And remember, Princess, no earthly father can ever fully take the place of your heavenly one. The King is your ultimate Dad—the One who will never leave, never fail, and never stop loving you.

 *Scripture Anchor:*
"See what kind of love the Father has given to us, that we should be called children of God; and so we are. The reason why the world does not know us is that it did not know him." (1 John 3:1)

Points to Ponder: How to Honor Your Dad

- Listen to His Wisdom: Dad's been around the block a few times, and his advice is often rooted in experience.

- Show Gratitude: A simple "thank you" for the little things can go a long way.

- Forgive His Faults: Just as The King forgives us, we're called to forgive others—even Dad.

- Pray for Him: Whether he's doing a great job or struggling, lift your Dad up in prayer. Ask The King to guide him, strengthen him, and draw him closer to The Kingdom.

Let's Bring It In

Dads are called to be providers, protectors, and leaders in their homes. They won't always get it right, but God asks us to honor them, thank them for the good they do, and forgive when they fall short. And for those who don't have a dad close by, remember, God Himself is the Father who never leaves. No matter what, we can trust Him to guide, protect, and love us perfectly.

But...What If I Don't Have A Mom or Dad?

Some of us grew up with bedtime stories and home-cooked meals. Some of us didn't. Some of us had parents who showed up. Some of us had to learn to survive without them.

Maybe your mom is gone. Maybe your dad walked out. Maybe you've never even met them. Maybe you're in foster care, bouncing between homes. Maybe you're trying to figure out why it feels like everyone always leaves.

If that's your story, this is for you.

You are not forgotten. You are not unwanted. You are not alone.

The Father Who Stays
(Come rain or shine)

Before anyone ever held you, He knew you.
Before anyone ever left you, He chose you.
God—The Father of Lights—has never looked away from you, not once. He sees every tear. Every birthday missed. Every question you've whispered in the dark.

He isn't like the people who broke your trust. He doesn't walk away. He doesn't change His mind. He is a Father to the fatherless, a refuge of peace and a safe place to land when the world feels too hard.

Family Looks Different Sometimes
(The blood of Jesus is all that matters)

God knows how to care for kids like you. He has a habit of writing redemption stories.
Sometimes He places you with the family you need, not the one you were born into. You may not have the same last names, but maybe sometimes it's about sharing something else... love.

He sends mentors. Teachers. Coaches. Church moms. Big brothers.
He sends grandmas with warm hugs, and neighbors who remember your name. God fills the gaps your parents may have left in your life in His own way and His own time... but you can trust that it will be good.

You may not have the traditional family story.
But you still have a story that matters.
And remember... God's not done with it yet.

You Are Loved By Name
(The Father doesn't make mistakes)

You're not a leftover.
Not an afterthought.
Not a mistake.

You are called by name.
You are crafted with purpose.
And you have a place in The Kingdom that no one else can fill.

So lift your head.
The King is not far off. He's right beside you.
And even if you never get the mom or dad you dreamed of,
you still get the best Father there is. Forever.

Siblings: Your Royal Allies (and Occasional Rivals)

Ah, siblings. One moment, they're your most trusted confidants, the next, they're borrowing your favorite crown (without asking!) or eating the last royal cookie. Siblings can be the greatest gift from The King—a built-in best friend and ally in life's adventures. But let's not pretend it's all sunshine and sparkles; sometimes, sharing a royal castle comes with its fair share of challenges.

Still, The King placed them in your life for a reason. They're there to teach you about love, patience, forgiveness, and the beauty of shared memories. So, let's dive into the magic (and occasional madness) of siblinghood!

> *Let's break it down, shall we?*

Why Siblings Matter

Siblings are like royal sidekicks. They're there to share in your joys, lend a hand in your struggles, and keep you grounded when you're tempted to let that crown go to your head. They've seen you at your best and your worst and still love you (even if they won't admit it).

But more importantly, siblings are part of The King's plan to shape you into the person He created you to be. Whether they're teaching you patience, challenging your perspective, or simply being there when no one else is, they're helping you grow in ways you might not even realize.

Scripture Anchor:
"As iron sharpens iron, so a man sharpens the countenance of his friend." (Proverbs 27:17)

The Challenges of Sharing the Castle

But siblings aren't always easy. They can be loud, annoying, and downright frustrating at times. Maybe they borrow your stuff without asking, tease you about the smallest things, or seem to always get away with stuff you'd never dream of doing.

But guess what? These challenges are part of The King's plan too. They teach you patience, grace, and how to love even when it's not easy. And when you work through those tough moments, you're building a relationship that can stand the test of time.

Scripture Anchor:
"Behold, how good and how pleasant it is for brethren to dwell together in unity!" (Psalm 133:1)

When Siblings Don't Get Along

Not all sibling relationships feel magical, Princess. Sometimes, they're strained or even broken. If that's your story, take heart: The King sees you, and He's in the business of restoration. Pray for healing, ask The King for wisdom, and trust that He can bring peace to even the toughest situations.

And remember, forgiveness is the key to freedom. It doesn't mean pretending nothing happened, but it does mean releasing bitterness and choosing love.

Scripture Anchor:
"And be kind to one another, tenderhearted, forgiving one another, even as God in Christ forgave you." (Ephesians 4:32)

Points to Ponder: How to Love Siblings

- Show Grace: Your siblings are human, just like you. They'll make mistakes, and so will you. Be quick to forgive and slow to hold grudges.

- Celebrate Their Wins: Jealousy is The Dragon's trap. When your sibling succeeds, cheer them on! Their victory doesn't diminish your value—it strengthens your royal family.

- Be Their Ally: Life is full of battles, and sometimes your sibling might need a partner in the fight. Stand by them, pray for them, and remind them they're never alone.

- Communicate with Kindness: Instead of snapping or rolling your eyes, talk it out. Let them know how you're feeling and be willing to listen too.

- Pray for Them: Nothing strengthens your bond more than lifting each other up to The King. Pray for their joys, their struggles, and their walk on The Way Road.

Let's Bring It In

Siblings are more than just the people you share a castle with—they're your co-adventurers, your memory-makers, and your biggest allies in the kingdom. Sure, there will be disagreements, but there will also be laughter, late-night talks, and the kind of bond that only comes from growing up together.

Cherish your siblings. Love them regardless, forgive them often, and thank The King for the gift they are. After all, they're the only ones who truly know what it's like to grow up in your unique royal story.

Grandparents: The Wise Wizards of the World

Oh, Princess, if life were a storybook, grandparents would undoubtedly be the wizards of wisdom. They're the keepers of stories, the holders of secrets, and the givers of hugs so magical, they could melt even the grumpiest dragon's icy heart. Grandparents have seen more seasons than you can imagine, and with each passing year, they've gathered wisdom like treasures in a royal vault.

So let's talk about why these incredible souls are such a gift from The King.

> Let's break it down, shall we?

The Gift of Experience

Grandparents have lived through it all—joys and sorrows, triumphs and trials. They've faced dragons of their own and come out the other side with lessons to share. Their advice, though sometimes wrapped in quirky sayings or old-fashioned logic, is like gold mined from the depths of life's hardest moments.

When they tell you to "be patient," or "save for a rainy day," they're not just being cautious—they're passing down the wisdom that kept them steady on The Way Road. Listening to their stories and heeding their advice can help you avoid pitfalls they've already overcome.

"Getting wisdom is the wisest thing you can do! And whatever else you do, develop good judgment." (Proverbs 4:7)

The Masters of Love

There's a reason grandparents are so quick to offer a plate of cookies or a big, warm hug—they've learned that love is the greatest legacy. Whether they spoil you with affection or quietly cheer you on, grandparents reflect The King's unconditional love.

They see you not for your flaws or mistakes but for the incredible person you're becoming.
They remind you that love isn't about perfection; it's about showing up, forgiving often, and pouring into others generously.

Scripture Anchor:
"Children's children are a crown to the aged, and parents are the pride of their children." (Proverbs 17:6)

The Value of Their Stories

Grandparents are living history books, Princess. The tales they tell about "back in the day" may seem like distant folklore, but within those stories are lessons of resilience, faith, and hope. Take the time to listen. Ask questions. Write their stories down if you can. Their lives are a testimony to The King's faithfulness, even through the toughest battles.

Scripture Anchor:
"Wisdom belongs to the aged and understanding to the old." (Job 12:12)

When Grandparents Aren't Perfect

Not all grandparents feel like warm hugs and homemade cookies. Some may have their own struggles, flaws, or even strained relationships with the family. But even in those cases, The King can use them to teach you grace, forgiveness, and the power of prayer.

Remember, Princess, no one is perfect except The King Himself. Even the wise wizards of the world have their weaknesses. But The King can work all things for good—including your relationship with them.

Scripture Anchor:
"Bear with each other and forgive one another if any of you has a grievance against someone. Forgive as the Lord forgave you." (Colossians 3:13)

Points to Ponder: Honoring Grandparents

- Listen to Their Stories: Ask about their childhood, their challenges, and their triumphs. They'll feel valued, and you'll gain treasures of wisdom.

- Show Appreciation: Whether it's a simple thank-you or spending time with them, let them know you cherish their presence in your life.

- Learn from Them: Their life lessons can guide you on your own journey.

- Pray for Them: Lift them up in prayer, asking The King to bless and strengthen them.

- Love Them Well: Even a quick call or note can brighten their day.

Let's Bring It In

Princess, your grandparents are more than just wise wizards—they're part of your royal heritage. They've played a role in shaping your family's story, and they have so much to teach you about faith, resilience, and love. Whether they're cooking up your favorite meal, sharing tales of the past, or quietly praying for you, their presence is a gift from The King.

So treasure your time with them, learn from their wisdom, and let their love remind you of The King's everlasting faithfulness.

Godly Mentors: The King's Earthly Protectors

Princess, have you ever walked into a dark forest and felt a little lost? That's where pastors and spiritual mentors come in. They're like lanterns on The Way Road, shining a light ahead and helping you navigate the twists and turns of life. These wise guides are a gift from The King Himself, chosen to encourage, teach, and support you as you journey home.

While The King is the ultimate source of wisdom and guidance, pastors and mentors serve as His ambassadors, pointing you back to Him. So, let's explore why these amazing people matter and how they can help you grow.

Let's break it down, shall we?

Who Are Pastors & Spiritual Mentors?

Pastors are shepherds of The King's flock, tasked with teaching His Word, praying for His people, and providing spiritual care. Think of them as royal guides, equipped to help you understand and apply The King's instructions.

Spiritual mentors, on the other hand, are more personal guides. They might not stand at a pulpit, but they walk alongside you, offering wisdom, accountability, and encouragement. Whether it's a youth leader, a trusted friend, or even a parent, a mentor is someone who helps you stay on The Way Road.

Scripture Anchor:
"Then I will give you shepherds after my own heart, who will lead you with knowledge and understanding." (Jeremiah 3:15)

Why You Need Them

The journey of faith isn't one you're meant to take alone. Pastors and mentors provide insight, perspective, and prayerful support when you're facing challenges or doubts. They're there to:

- Teach You The King's Word: Pastors and mentors help you dive into scripture, unpack its treasures, and understand how it applies to your life.

- Keep You Accountable: A good mentor will lovingly challenge you to stay faithful, even when it's hard.

- Encourage You in Tough Times: They remind you of The King's promises and help you see the bigger picture when life feels overwhelming.

- Model Faithfulness: By watching their lives, you can learn what it looks like to walk closely with The King.

Scripture Anchor:
"Therefore encourage one another and build each other up, just as in fact you are doing." (1 Thessalonians 5:11)

Points to Ponder

- Be Teachable : Approach your pastor or mentor with a humble heart, ready to learn. The King works through them to guide you, so listen with an open mind and a willing spirit.

- Ask Questions: Don't be afraid to seek clarity or share your struggles. Mentors are there to help you grow, and they'll appreciate your honesty.

- Pray for Them: Pastors and mentors pour so much into others —it's important to lift them up in prayer too. Ask The King to strengthen, encourage, and guide them as they lead.

- Show Gratitude: A simple thank-you note or kind word can mean the world to someone who's dedicated to serving you and The Kingdom.

Let's Bring It In

God gives us pastors, spiritual mentors, and wise guides to help us on The Way Road. They aren't perfect, but they shine light, give perspective, and point us back to Him when we feel lost. These mentors protect us with prayer, strengthen us with encouragement, and remind us of The King's truth.

When we listen, ask questions, and show gratitude, we grow stronger and wiser for The Kingdom. Their care is a gift from God, and their faithfulness points us to The King's everlasting faithfulness.

Best Friends: Choosing Your Royal Court

Every princess needs her royal court—a squad of trusted allies who will laugh with you, cry with you, and maybe even tell you when your crown is on crooked. Friends are a big deal. Like, huge. Think of them as the soldiers who guard your heart and the jesters who keep your life fun. But, spoiler alert: not everyone deserves a spot at your royal round table.

Some friends lift you up; others drag you down. And some... well, let's just say they've got more drama than a Disney villain. Choosing the right court is about finding people who reflect The King's love, speak truth, and inspire you to be your best and brightest self. Ready to find your crew? Let's dive into five ways to know who belongs in your royal court.

Let's break it down, shall we?

They Cheer for Your Wins
(And Stick Around for Your Losses)

A true royal friend celebrates your victories without a hint of jealousy. Got an A on that test you thought you'd bomb? They're clapping. Made the soccer team or got the part in the play? They're your loudest cheerleader and your best audience. And when life throws you a plot twist, they're there too—offering tissues, hugs, or just their silent presence. Fake friends disappear when things get tough; real friends dig in and stay.

 *Scripture Anchor:*
"Rejoice with those who rejoice; mourn with those who mourn." (Romans 12:15)

They Tell You the Truth
(Even When It's Hard)

Sometimes, love looks like honesty. If your attitude stinks, your real friends won't let you wallow in it. If you're about to make a bad choice, they'll lovingly pull you back. Truth-tellers aren't about tearing you down—they're about helping you grow. Remember, iron sharpens iron, and good friends make you sharper, not duller.

 *Scripture Anchor:*
"Faithful are the wounds of a friend, but the kisses of an enemy are deceitful." (Proverbs 27:6)

They're Givers, Not Takers
(They're Not Black Holes Sucking You Dry)

Royal friends don't drain your emotional tank; they fill it. Sure, friendships are about giving and taking, but if someone always expects you to drop everything for them and never returns the favor? That's not balance; that's a one-sided deal. Look for friends who serve, share, and pour into your life as much as you pour into theirs.

Scripture Anchor:
"Don't waste what is holy on people who are unholy. Don't throw your pearls to pigs! They will trample the pearls, then turn and attack you." (Matthew 7:6)

They Point You Back to The King
(Because They Are On The Way Road Too)

The best kind of friends don't just walk with you through everything—they keep your eyes on God through it all. When life gets hard, they remind you to pray. When you win, they praise God with you. When you cry, they remind you that God still sees you. And when things change, they point you back to the One who never does... Your Father In Heaven!

Scripture Anchor:
"So encourage each other and build each other up, just as you are already doing."
(1 Thessalonians 5:11)

What If Your Court Is Pulling You Down
(Like Crabs in a Barrel)

Ever heard of the "crabs in a barrel" effect? It's what happens when one crab tries to climb out—and the others pull it back down. Some friendships work the same way. Instead of cheering for your growth, they grip tighter, pull you back into old habits, or guilt you for wanting more. But royalty doesn't stay stuck. You were made to rise.

If your current crew is more about drama, gossip, or dragging you away from The Kingdom... it might be time for a royal makeover. That doesn't necessarily mean ghosting them—but it does means setting boundaries, praying for them, and asking The King to bring the right people into your life. Trust Him; He's got your court all planned out.

Remember, Princess, your friends are like mirrors. The right ones will reflect the truth about who you are: chosen, loved, and priceless. So, choose your royal court wisely. And don't forget to have fun along the way—because life with good friends? It's an adventure worth taking.

Scripture Anchor:
"Walk with the wise and become wise, for a companion of fools suffers harm" (Proverbs 13:20)

Points to Ponder

- Do your friends celebrate your wins—or do they go quiet when good things happen for you?

- When life gets messy, who shows up and who disappears?

- Can your friends call you out with love? And can you receive it without getting defensive?

- Do your friends pour back into you—or do they only reach out when they need something?

- Are you being the kind of friend you want to have?

- Have you asked The King to bring the right people into your life—or are you still trying to do the picking on your own?

Let's Bring It In

"Do not be deceived: 'Bad company ruins good morals.'"
(1 Corinthians 15:33)

Mic Drop.

7

Growing Up

One minute you're climbing trees and having snack time, and the next... BAM!!!

You're staring in the mirror wondering who that person is looking back. Body changes, mood swings, comparison traps, awkward growth spurts, late-night questions, and the pressure to present a perfect version of yourself online—it's all part of the wild ride called growing up.

But this chapter isn't about surviving it—it's about understanding it, owning it, and walking through it with wisdom. Let's get ready to talk about the tough stuff: hormones, modesty, identity, social media and more. It's time to learn how to face it all with grace, truth, and the confidence of a daughter who knows that her worth comes from her Father, not from what she sees while scrolling on her phone.

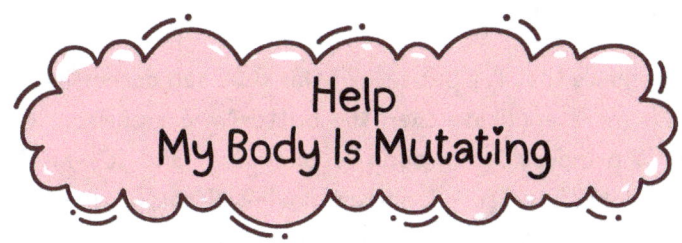

Help
My Body Is Mutating

We've all heard the analogy of puberty being like the metamorphosis of a caterpillar to a butterfly. We can hear in our minds the classical piano playing as we imagine the magnificent monarch as it appears from her cocoon. (Exhaling with reverence) Ah, the beauty of nature... NOT!!! This analogy couldn't be further from the truth. Let's paint the real picture, shall we?

Imagine you're walking down Main Street at night. The silvery glow of the moon shines brightly upon your face. You breathe in the crisp air as the click-clap of your shoes prance across the concrete. All is well. Until...

RIP! You hear the sound of your clothes shred as your limbs begin to bulge and your core begins to sprout! Hair like an animal covers you all over as a crazed look takes over your eyes... You're a monster!

(Dramatic pause)

There. How's that for puberty? I think we can agree that this sounds more accurate than the butterfly comparison. Let's face it princess: your body is changing, and it's kind of weird, right? Even sci-fi, horror-movie weird! One day you're just going about your life, and the next, your reflection is like, "Who is this person?"

Things are stretching, growing, and sprouting in places that were once totally predictable. Suddenly, you're hyper-aware of your body, and maybe, just maybe, you're feeling a little awkward or even ashamed.

But here's the truth: these changes aren't accidents. They're part of The King's intricate design, preparing your body for the incredible journey ahead. Yes, it's strange and sometimes uncomfortable, but it's also beautiful. You're not losing yourself—you're growing into who you were always meant to be. So let's break it down, one change at a time, and see if we can't turn some of that awkwardness into awe.

Let's break it down, shall we?

Growing Curves
The New Landscape

Let's start with the obvious: your body is gaining curves. Your hips might be widening, your chest is developing, and your waist is starting to define itself. This can feel exciting, but it can also feel really weird. Suddenly, clothes fit differently, people might comment on your "grown-up" look, and you're hyper-aware of your silhouette.

Here's what you need to know: these changes are completely normal. Your body is preparing for its next stage of life, and that includes a shape that's strong and capable. Those hips? They're built to support you through whatever adventures The Way Road has in store. And yes, bras are a thing now. Whether you're excited about them or totally confused, remember that they're just part of the royal wardrobe upgrade. This new shape is meant to bear the weight of all the battles and beauty this new season has to offer.

Scripture Anchor:
"Thank you for making me so wonderfully complex! Your workmanship is marvelous—how well I know it." (Psalm 139:14)

Hair in New Places
The Uninvited Guest

Ah, yes, the hair. It's showing up under your arms, on your legs, and in other places you probably didn't expect. It might even feel like you're turning into a werewolf. It can feel embarrassing at first, but don't worry—it's just your body's way of saying, "Hey, I'm growing up!"

You get to decide how to handle this new arrival. Some princesses embrace it, others choose to shave or wax—it's totally up to you. Just remember, this hair isn't something to be ashamed of. It's a natural, normal part of puberty that every princess deals with. If you're unsure how to manage it, don't be afraid to ask someone you trust for advice.

Skin Drama
Breakouts and Oil Patrol

Oh, the joys of teenage skin. Your once smooth complexion might now be waging a full-blown rebellion. Pimples, blackheads, and oily skin can feel like little orcs sprouting out of your face. And you're thinking, "I used to be beautiful! I used to be cute! It just doesn't seem fair!" But fear not. This too shall pass. Acne is just your hormones doing their thing.

This doesn't mean you're dirty or doing something wrong—it just means your skin needs a little extra care now. Wash your face regularly, eat balanced meals, and don't stress if your skin isn't "perfect." Even royalty deals with breakouts now and then. And when it feels like too much, remember: The King sees your heart, not your pimples.

Periods
The Monthly Milestone

Let's not forget the big one: your period. This is the moment when your body starts preparing for the possibility of creating life someday (way, way in the future, Princess—don't worry). It can feel overwhelming at first, and look like the scene of a crime—especially when you're trying to figure out pads and tampons. And the cramps! Well, they make you wonder if someone shrunk a team of dart throwers and put them in your stomach to compete for the final tournament—not fun.

But your period is also a sign of health and strength. It's your body saying, "I'm working exactly as I was designed to." Talk to your mom or a female mentor you trust about how to handle it, and remember, you're not alone—every princess navigates this new normal.

Scripture Anchor:
"There is a time for everything, and a season for every activity under the heavens." (Ecclesiastes 3:1)

Points to Ponder

- Do I believe that my body is beautiful—even in the changes I don't fully understand yet?

- Am I giving myself the same grace I'd give a friend who feels awkward or unsure?

- What questions am I too afraid or embarrassed to ask—and who can I go to that's safe and wise?

- Am I recognizing the strength in my body, even when it feels uncomfortable or unfamiliar?

- Do I realize I'm not the only one on this path—that I'm part of a whole sisterhood walking it with me?

Let's Bring It In

Princess, puberty is awkward, weird, and sometimes downright scary, but it's also a beautiful season of growth. Your body is changing, not because it's flawed, but because it's becoming stronger, more capable, and ready for the incredible journey ahead.

So when you feel overwhelmed, lean on The King. He sees you, loves you, and is walking with you through every awkward step. You're not just growing up—you're growing into the woman He created you to be. And that, Princess, is something worth celebrating.

Wearing Make Up

Ah, makeup—the royal toolkit of powders, brushes, and magical potions that can take you from "just rolled out of bed" to "ready for the royal ball" in ten minutes flat. It's like a box of crayons for your face, and let's be honest: it's fun to play with! A little eyeliner here, a dab of blush there, and suddenly, you're looking like you slept eight hours (even if you didn't).

But here's the deal, Princess: makeup is like the sprinkles on the ice-cream sunday. It's a highlight, not the headline. The Dragon would love for you to think that your worth is measured by your mascara game, but The King? He's already declared you radiant—with or without lipstick.

So, grab your brushes, your confidence, and maybe that favorite lip gloss, and let's talk about how to rock makeup in a way that lets your true beauty shine through.

> *Let's break it down, shall we?*

Makeup: A Tool, Not Your Treasure

First things first: makeup isn't the problem. It's your heart behind it that matters. Are you using it to enhance the beauty God already gave you, or are you hiding behind it like a mask? Makeup can be fun, creative, and a form of self-expression, but it should never define your worth.

The King already calls you beautiful. He designed you, after all! Your freckles, your dimples, your unique quirks—those are His masterpieces. Makeup is like adding a bit of sparkle to an already stunning crown. It's not the crown itself.

Scripture Anchor:
"The Lord does not look at the things people look at. People look at the outward appearance, but the Lord looks at the heart." (1 Samuel 16:7)

Why Are You Wearing It?

Let's get real for a second: why do you reach for that mascara or brush on that blush? Is it because it makes you feel confident, or because you're worried people won't like you without it? The King wants you to know that your value isn't found in how perfectly winged your eyeliner is. It's found in Him.

Makeup can be a fun way to express yourself, but it shouldn't become an idol or a shield. If you're wearing it to impress others or to chase their approval, it's time to hit pause and ask The King to remind you of your true beauty.

Scripture Anchor:
"Those who look to Him are radiant; their faces are never covered with shame." (Psalm 34:5)

Makeup: Enhancement, Not Enchantment

Let's talk about those wild makeup makeovers—the ones that can turn you into a completely different person. You know the kind: a 20-minute tutorial promises to transform your face so much that even your own reflection might do a double take. The Dragon loves to sell the lie that if you could just "fix" your face—bigger eyes, fuller lips, higher cheekbones... or even just a different body altogether—then you'd finally be beautiful.

But here's the truth: you're not a blank slate waiting to be rewritten—you are a masterpiece crafted by The King. Makeup should enhance the beauty that's already there, not enchant you into thinking you need to look like someone else. The King didn't design you to be a copy of the latest beauty trend; He created you with purpose, down to every freckle, smile line, and sparkle in your eyes.

So go ahead, experiment with colors and styles—makeup is fun! But remember, Princess, the real magic is in your heart, not your highlighter.

Scripture Anchor:
"Yet God has made everything beautiful for its own time."
(Ecclesiastes 3:11)

Points to Ponder

- Am I letting makeup complement who I am—or is it starting to cover me up?

- Before I reach for the mascara or lip gloss, have I checked in with my heart and asked why I'm putting it on?

- Am I using makeup to celebrate my natural beauty, or to hide the things I haven't learned to love yet?

- Is my creativity shining—or is my confidence depending too much on how I look?

- What's the real glow people see when they look at me—my highlight, or the light of The King reflected in my actions and love?

Let's Bring It In

Makeup and style can be fun, but they were never meant to define your worth. God reminds us that true beauty comes from a gentle and faithful heart, not from what's on the surface. Makeup should be a tool that enhances—not a mask that hides. The way we dress and present ourselves should honor God, respect our bodies, and point others toward The King, not away from Him.

When we let modesty, wisdom, and confidence in Christ guide our choices, our outside can reflect the beauty that's already inside. Princess, you are already treasured and radiant in The King's eyes.

Moo Moos and Modesty

Modesty—a word that might make you roll your eyes and think of your grandma's closet or those medieval dresses that look like they were sewn by candlelight. But hang on, Princess! Modesty isn't about becoming a walking quilt or renouncing jeans forever.

It's about owning your look in a way that screams, "I know my worth, and I don't need flashing lights to prove it!"

Let's break it down, shall we?

Your Wardrobe Is Speaking
What's It Saying?

Your outfit starts the conversation before you do. It's like walking into a room with a giant speech bubble over your head that says, "This is me!" The Dragon would love for your wardrobe to shout things like, "Please notice me!" or "I'll do anything to fit in!"

But The King's message is entirely different. He wants your outfit to reflect the confidence, grace, and beauty that come from knowing exactly who you are.

Here's the truth, Princess: if you're dressing in a way that leaves nothing to the imagination, you might get attention—but not the kind you deserve. Respect is built on character, kindness, and confidence—not on how much skin you show.

And let's just be real, showing all your bits through a low-cut shirt and exposing all your curves in a bip-bop skirt is NOT the vibe. The right people (and yes, we're talking about guys too) will admire you for who you are, not for what you're wearing.

Modesty lets the real you shine, making sure you're seen for your heart, not just your outfit. And let's be honest: a little mystery is far more intriguing than putting it all out there.

Scripture Anchor:

"Your beauty should not come from outward adornment... Rather, it should be that of your inner self, the unfading beauty of a gentle and quiet spirit, which is of great worth in God's sight." (1 Peter 3:3-4)

The Freedom of Modesty

Here's the twist no one tells you: modesty is less about restrictions and more about freedom. When you embrace modesty, you're saying goodbye to the pressure to conform to trends, show off to fit in, or seek validation through your wardrobe. Instead, you're free to be yourself—creative, confident, and comfortable in your own skin.

And let's be honest: too-short skirts and too-tight tops aren't just uncomfortable—they're disasters waiting to happen. Ever spent an entire evening pulling down your hemline every time you stood up? Or awkwardly crossing your arms because your shirt decided to be less "shirt" and more "surprise!"? Modesty lets you sidestep those moments entirely. It's like having a wardrobe that works with you instead of against you.

When you embrace modesty, you're free to walk into a room without a single tug, pull, or awkward shuffle. You can focus on what really matters—your character, your kindness, and your confidence. It's not about shrinking—it's about standing tall, secure in the knowledge that you're already enough. And trust me, nothing shines brighter than that.

Scripture Anchor:

"She is clothed with strength and dignity; she can laugh at the days to come." (Proverbs 31:25)

Style + Modesty = Perfection

Here's the good news: modesty doesn't mean you have to trade your style for a shapeless sack. In fact, modesty and style are best friends when you do it right. You get to be creative, expressive, and fashion forward—all while dressing in a way that reflects your royal identity.

Here's how to rock modesty like the trendsetter you are:

- Flattering, Not Flaunting: Choose clothes that highlight your beauty without shouting for attention. Think elegant and chic, not tight and tiny.

- Layers Are Your Best Friend: A cute jacket or stylish scarf can turn any outfit into a modest masterpiece. Plus, layers = instant cozy vibes.

- Accessorize With Intent: Jewelry, belts, and shoes can add sparkle and flair without revealing more than you'd want.

- Be Confident: The best accessory is your attitude. When you wear confidence, you outshine even the most dazzling outfit.

Remember, Princess: you're not dressing to blend in or to compete. You're dressing to reflect your worth as a daughter of The King.

Scripture Anchor:
"So whether you eat or drink or whatever you do, do it all for the glory of God." (1 Corinthians 10:31)

Points to Ponder

- What's your outfit saying about you? Think about how your wardrobe reflects your confidence and identity.

- Are you dressing for approval or authenticity? Ask yourself if your style choices reflect The King's truth about your worth or the world's expectations.

- How does modesty set you free? Consider how modesty can release you from the pressure of trends and let you embrace true confidence.

- What's your modesty masterpiece? Celebrate the outfits that make you feel beautiful while staying true to your royal values.

- How can your style inspire others? Use your wardrobe to encourage others to embrace modesty and grace in their own way.

Let's Bring It In

Modesty isn't about hiding—it's about shining for the right reasons. The King isn't measuring your hemlines—He's looking at your heart. When you embrace modesty, you're showing the world that you know your worth comes from Him, not from what you wear. So, Princess, throw on your favorite modest masterpiece, add a dash of confidence, and go shine like the royal you are.

Social Media
Is It Okay?

Ah, social media—a glittering palace of selfies, stories, and endless scrolls. It's where you can share your royal adventures, keep up with friends, and discover new things. But let's not forget: it's also where The Dragon loves to attack. Whether it's the trap of comparison, the lure of distractions, or the temptation to find your worth in likes and comments, social media can be as tricky as a maze without a map.

Fear not, Princess. The King has given you wisdom to shine in this digital world without losing your way. Let's explore how to use social media as a tool for good while staying true to your royal identity.

Let's break it down, shall we?

What's Social Media Really About?

At its best, social media is like a royal banquet where everyone brings their best stories, photos, and ideas to share. It's a way to connect, encourage, and even spread The King's love to far corners of the kingdom.

But at its worst, it can become a hall of mirrors, reflecting distorted images that lead to envy, self-doubt, or even unkindness. The Dragon loves to use social media to whisper lies like "You're not enough" or "You'll only matter if they like your post."

The truth? Your worth isn't found in a filter, a follower count, or the perfect caption. It's found in The King.

Scripture Anchor:

"Am I now trying to win the approval of human beings, or of God? Or am I trying to please people? If I were still trying to please people, I wouldn't be a servant of Christ." (Galatians 1:10)

When Social Media Gets Messy

Even the best princesses can feel overwhelmed by the digital world. Maybe you're scrolling and suddenly feel not-enough-itis creeping in. Or perhaps a comment stings, and you start to question yourself.

When that happens, stop. Close the app. Take a deep breath and talk to The King. Ask Him to remind you of your worth, to help you forgive, and to guide your heart. If the situation is serious enough, talk to someone (a parent or mentor). Maybe even take a break from the screen for a while.
Remember: your value isn't in your posts, your followers, or your likes. It's in The King's unwavering love for you.

Scripture Anchor:

"Do not conform to the pattern of this world, but be transformed by the renewing of your mind..." (Romans 12:2)

Points to Ponder

- Remember Who You Are. Before you hit "post," remember: you're a daughter of The King. Your online presence should reflect His light and love. Ask yourself, "Does this post honor Him? Does it encourage or uplift?"

- Don't Compare Your Behind-the-Scenes to Their Highlight Reel. People share the best parts of their lives online, not the messy middle. Comparing your real life to their curated posts is like comparing a royal feast to an appetizer—it's incomplete and unfair.

- Be a Kindhearted Queen. Your words, whether typed or spoken, hold power. Use them to build up, not tear down. Leave comments that encourage, share posts that inspire, and resist the urge to join in drama or gossip.

- Set Healthy Boundaries. Social media is fun, but it can't replace real-life connections or time with The King. Limit your screen time, take breaks when needed, and make space for prayer, reading the Word, and spending time with loved ones.

- Use It for Good. Social media can be a powerful tool to share hope, truth, and love. Post Bible verses, encourage someone having a hard day, or share how The King is working in your life. Let your profile be a reflection of His light.

Social media is a tool, not a throne. Use it wisely, Princess. Let it be a space where you reflect The King's love, encourage others, and share your story with purpose. But don't let it consume your time, steal your joy, or define your worth.

At the end of the day, The King sees you—not through a filter, but just as you are. And He delights in the real, unfiltered, beautifully unique person He created.

So post that picture, share that story, and like your friend's post—but do it all with grace, kindness, and the confidence that comes from being a daughter of The King.

Before We Go Any Further...
Let's Make Sure You're Truly Awake

Is your heart resonating with any of this? Or are you just flipping pages from one doodle drawing to the next?

If for some reason, you're still seeing Dystopia as Heaven on Earth... If The Way Road that leads away from the sin of this world isn't shining in front of you... if your steps haven't felt the pull of the Father's voice yet... That means The Dragon's curse still has a hold on you... And you are still asleep. And we need to deal with that first.

So... Let me ask you something: Do you know where you stand with Your Father in Heaven, aka God? Has there ever been a moment when you gave Him your whole heart?

Because until that happens... you're still living under the curse. Freedom doesn't come from pretending the world is fine. It comes from seeing that it's not—and knowing you need a Savior.

So let's recap your predicament real quick, wake you up, and get you on The Way Road.

 # Recap

You were made by a King, aka The Father of Lights, Creator of Heaven and Earth. He made you with love and in a perfect world. But an evil dragon, aka Satan, tricked you and placed the curse of this evil world on you. That's where we get sin, pain, and death from.

There was no way out of this mess. You were cursed to live in fear, pain, and sin forever. No one could pay the perfect debt to get you out... NO ONE. Until Your Father sent His Savior... aka Part of the God Trinity, aka God's Only Begotten Son, aka Jesus.

God literally stepped off His throne and came down here to this nightmare world to pay the price for you... so that your eyes could be opened... so that you can come home back home.

Jesus—God in the flesh, The White Knight Himself—walked the dirt roads, healed the broken, and lived the perfect life we couldn't.
Then He did what no one else could do...

He took the curse for us.

On a wooden cross, He bore every shame, every wound, every lie we ever believed. He let The Dragon strike Him down. He shed His blood and died... God's only son DIED! Let that sink in.
But... three days later—He rose again and CRUSHED The Dragon and carved a road back to your Father in Heaven.

But here's the catch...

You can't receive this gift unless you Accept it.

ACCEPT HIM... JESUS—the Father's gift to you... your Savior.

 # How to say yes to Jesus

- Believe that Jesus is the Savior of the world—
  the One who died for your sins and rose again.

- Repent—which means to turn around.
  Leave The Dragon's lies behind and walk toward The King.

- Receive His forgiveness. You don't have to earn it.
  Just receive it with open hands and a surrendered heart.

- Follow Him—not perfectly, but fully.
  The Helper will walk with you every step from here on out.

It's that simple

God doesn't need you to be perfect to reach your heart

He just needs your heart... then HE will perfect you.

☑ Pray This (If You're Ready)

Lord Jesus, I know I need You.
I've been trying to do life my way, but it's empty.
I believe You died for me, took my sin, and rose again.

Please forgive me of my sins.
Become Lord and Master over my life.
Make me a daughter of God, the way I was meant to be.

You say in Your Word that You are "The Way, The Truth, and The Life,"
and that no one comes to the Father but by You.
So I submit my life to You.

I need You to show me the way that I should go.
Fill me with Your Truth.
And breathe life into me by Your Spirit.

Today I give You my heart. I give You my life.
I'm Yours. Forever.
Amen.

OOO

☑ Now Breathe

If you meant that—welcome home, daughter.
The curse is broken. The road is open.
The Father of Lights sees you.
The White Knight has saved you.
And The Helper will never leave your side.
Your Father's Kingdom is waiting.

Let's Go!

8
Matters of the Heart

Love. Crushes. Flirting. Dating.
Courtship. Purity.

Yeah, we're going there, Princess. Because the heart is tender, and the world is loud—and somewhere between butterflies and bad decisions, we need some holy clarity. This chapter isn't here to shame you or hand you a list of do's and don'ts. It's here to help you guard what's sacred, honor The King in how you love, and figure out what it really means to walk wisely when feelings start flying.

What Does Purity Really Mean?

Let's talk about your royal heart—the very core of who you are. In The Kingdom of Lights, it's the most precious thing you own. And like all valuable treasures, it needs protection. Think of it like guarding the gates of a castle. Not everyone or everything deserves a key.

The Dragon loves to sneak in and whisper lies, like "Everyone's doing it," or "It's no big deal." Lies, all lies. Your Father knows that He created this part of you for something special... for *someone* special. So, staying pure in your thoughts, actions, and relationships keeps you spotless as you wait for that special guy your Father will reveal to you—when the time is right.

But let's get real: choosing purity isn't always easy. Sometimes it feels like swimming against a tide of glittery temptation and peer pressure. That's why The King gave you His Spirit—The Helper—to guide and strengthen you. When you feel weak, ask the Helper for help. He's like a knight standing guard at your castle gates.

Dating vs Courting

Love? It's a big deal. It's the kind of thing that gets your heart racing, your palms sweaty, and your dreams spinning with possibilities. But here's the thing: not all love stories are created equal. And as a royal daughter of The King, your heart isn't something to be spent on casual whims—it's a treasure meant to be guarded, nurtured, and offered with purpose. That's where the difference between dating and courtship comes in.

Let's break it down, shall we?

Dating:
The Casual Expenditure

Dating is like grocery shopping when you're starving. Everything looks good, even the stuff you'd normally never grab. You fill your cart with feelings and moments, but by the time you get to checkout, you're holding a receipt for things you didn't need—and maybe a stomachache too.
Picture this:

You meet him in 3rd period Biology. He sits diagonally across from you, always doodling dramatic lightning bolts on his worksheet and pretending the classroom skeleton is waving at you. One day he drops a note on your desk that just says, "Biology is better with you."

You roll your eyes. You smirk. You laugh. And, well… something shifts.

Suddenly, he's messaging you "good morning" before group study and walking with you to lunch afterward. It's not technically a relationship, but it's definitely a thing. You're smiling at your phone more. Your friends are teasing you (in the fun way). You start planning your outfits for Biology days. It's nice and you like the way this makes you feel.

129

But slowly, it shifts. His texts slow down. His jokes don't land the same. You spot him talking to someone else near the lockers and your stomach does a weird backflip. You finally work up the courage to ask him what's going on between you two—what this *thing* between you guys really *is*. But he just shrugs and says, "Nothing. We're just friends, right?"

And you? You're now emotionally invested in someone who treats your heart like a group project—they show up when it's convenient, but never really commit.

Dating says, "Let's just see what happens." But without direction, it's easy to end up wandering. And wandering hearts get tired fast. You weren't made for that kind of emotional scavenger hunt. You're not a science experiment. You're a daughter of The King—with a heart too precious for guesswork.

Scripture Anchor:
"Above all else, guard your heart, for everything you do flows from it." (Proverbs 4:23)

Courtship:
The Intentional Journey

Courtship is like planting a garden. You don't toss seeds and hope for the best—you clear space, check the weather, follow the instructions, and water it daily. You're growing something on purpose, not just hoping it magically blooms.

Here's what that might look like:

There's this guy from youth group—let's call him... *Johny*. You've known him for a while. He always volunteers for cleanup, laughs at dad jokes, and actually prays when people say, "Let's pray." One night after small group, he tells your youth leader, "I'd like to get to know her (you) better—but I want to do it the right way." (Yes, that actually happens.)

Your parents know. His parents know. Nobody's hiding anything. You still hang out in groups—board game night, worship night, nacho night (because... obviously). You talk about real stuff: faith, family, what you want your futures to look like. He asks about your dreams, not just your favorite pizza topping.

You text—but it's not *wyd* at 1am. It's "Hey, I read something in Psalms and thought of you." You set boundaries early. You pray together—but not alone in dark corners. You both agree not to rush anything because you'd rather grow something real than fake something fast.

Courtship says, "I'm not here to borrow your heart. I'm here to honor it—whether this leads to marriage or simply teaches us both how to love like Jesus."

It's not a checklist. It's a mindset. A sacred pause in a world that rushes. It's not stiff or awkward—it's peaceful. Because when you date with purpose, you're not chasing butterflies. You're planting roots.

Scripture Anchor:

"Do not arouse or awaken love until it so desires."
(Song of Songs 2:7) → *Translation: don't microwave what God intended to slow-cook.*

Points to Ponder

 ### Secret vs. Seen

- Dating often happens in secret: late-night texts, "just hanging out," no real plan. It can feel thrilling—but also lonely, like something you can't talk about openly.

- Courtship brings the light in. It invites trusted adults—parents, mentors, youth leaders—into the journey. Not for control, but for covering. Love doesn't need to hide.

Vibes vs. Vision

- Dating is usually based on chemistry, looks, or how they make you feel in the moment.

- Courtship starts with character. Do they love Jesus? Can they lead or walk beside you in faith? Do they see your calling and not just your cuteness?

 Playing House vs. Building Foundation

- Dating can feel like a mini-marriage with none of the covenant. Sharing deep emotions, physical affection, or even spiritual intimacy too soon can create false bonds.

- Courtship honors timing. It builds a foundation of friendship, shared faith, and mutual respect—before things get romantic. It says, "Let's build something real. But let's build it right."

How Far Can We Go? vs. How Holy Can We Stay?"

- Dating often asks, "What's the limit?" and plays as close to the line as possible.

- Courtship flips the question. It asks, "What helps us honor God?" It chooses boundaries out of love, not restriction—because purity isn't about shame. It's about worth.

Temporary vs. Eternal Mindset

- Dating often ends with a shrug: "Well, that didn't work out."

- Courtship doesn't promise a perfect outcome, but it promises a purposeful one. Whether the relationship leads to marriage or not, it leaves you wiser, not wounded—closer to God, not further.

Let's Bring It In

Not all love stories are created equal.
Dating without purpose can feel fun in the moment—but it often leaves behind confusion, heartbreak, and pieces of your heart scattered in places they were never meant to stay. It's a journey with no map and no destination.

Courtship is different. It's love with a compass. It's intentional, prayerful, and centered on God's plan—not just feelings. And it has a clear destination: marriage. Not just a wedding—but a lifelong covenant, built on trust, faith, and the kind of love that lasts.

Crushes & Flirting
Is It Okay?

Oh, Princess, let's talk about those *heart-fluttering*, *stomach-butterflies*, can't help but *doodle-his-name-on-your-notebook* moments. You know what I mean... crushes. They're exciting, overwhelming, and sometimes downright confusing. Add a dash of flirting to the mix, and suddenly, you've got a recipe for potential royal mischief. But fear not! We're here to navigate these waters with the wisdom of The King and just the right amount of sparkle.

Let's break it down, shall we?

Crushes:
When Your Heart Says "Oooh!"

First, let's normalize it: having a crush is totally okay. Your heart is wired to notice beauty, kindness, and strength in the opposite sex. That's a gift from The King! But here's the thing—a crush is kind of like finding a treasure map. It might be exciting, but you don't drop everything and chase it without thinking. Crushes need to be handled with wisdom and grace.

When you feel that spark of admiration, pause for a royal reality check. Ask yourself:

- Do I admire this person for who they are, or am I caught up in their charm?

- Am I seeing them through The King's eyes or through a filter of daydreams and social media?

- Is this feeling leading me closer to God, or is it distracting me from my journey?

Remember, a crush isn't a calling—it's just a whisper. It's okay to feel the flutter, as long as your heart stays anchored in truth and your feet keep walking The Way Road.

Scripture Anchor:
"Desire without knowledge is not good—how much more will hasty feet miss the way!" (Proverbs 19:2)

Flirting:
Playful or Problematic?

Now, let's talk about flirting. It's fun, right? A cheeky smile here, a clever comment there... it's all part of the game. But is it a game worth playing? The King calls His daughters to a higher standard—one where our words and actions reflect His love, not just our own interests. Flirting might feel innocent, but it's like waving a shiny object around without knowing its true effect.

Here's a royal truth bomb: Flirting can send mixed messages, stir up emotions prematurely, and even hurt others unintentionally. As The King's daughter, your words and actions carry weight. They should be used to uplift, not confuse. Ask yourself:

- Am I flirting to get attention, or am I genuinely building a connection?

- Would I act this way if The King Himself were watching? (Spoiler: He is.)

- Am I honoring the person I'm flirting with, or am I leading them astray?

Scripture Anchor:
"Do not let any unwholesome talk come out of your mouths, but only what is helpful for building others up... that it may benefit those who listen." (Ephesians 4:29)

The Royal Standard:
Admiration with Honor

Here's the deal: crushes and compliments aren't bad, but they need to be anchored in respect and integrity. You can admire someone without turning it into a giggly, flirty show. Treat them as a fellow heir to The Kingdom of Lights, not just a character in your daydream.

Want to compliment someone? Go for it! But make sure your words are genuine and God-honoring. Instead of, "Wow, you're so hot," try, "You have such a kind and thoughtful heart" or "I admire how you serve others." (Bonus: This weeds out the frogs from the princes.)

Scripture Anchor:
"Love each other with genuine affection, and take delight in honoring each other." (Romans 12:10)

Points to Ponder

- Take It to The King: Pray about your feelings. Ask for wisdom, clarity, and guidance. The King knows your heart better than anyone else.

- Talk to Your Inner Court: Share your thoughts with a trusted mentor or friend who will offer godly advice.

- Guard Your Imagination: Daydreams are fun, but don't let them run wild. Keep your thoughts grounded in reality and God's truth.

- Focus on Friendship: Instead of obsessing over romantic possibilities, focus on building a respectful, Christ-centered friendship.

- Trust The King's Timing: If this crush is meant to blossom into something more, The King will make it clear in His perfect time.

Let's Bring It In

Princess, your heart is precious—a treasure designed for a purpose far greater than fleeting feelings. Crushes and flirting might feel fun and exciting, but they're just small chapters in your grand love story. Keep your eyes on The King, honor others with your actions, and trust that His plan for your relationships is better than anything you could dream up.

So go ahead and enjoy the butterflies, but remember who you are and whose you are. You're a daughter of The King... and that means you love with purpose, walk with integrity, and save your best for the one who's worthy of it.

What About Kissing?

Alright, Princess, let's tackle the big, blushing question: Is it okay to kiss before marriage? Whether you're daydreaming about that magical first kiss or wondering if you've already crossed a line, this topic can feel a little tricky. But don't worry, we're diving into it with all the grace, wisdom, and quirkiness you've come to expect. Ready? Let's go.

Let's break it down, shall we?

What's the Big Deal About Kissing?
Playful or Problematic?

A kiss isn't just a kiss. It's intimate, vulnerable, and powerful. When you kiss someone, you're not just sharing a moment—you're building a connection. And connections? They're serious business.

The question isn't so much *can* you kiss before marriage but *should* you. Will this act honor The King? Or will it cloud your judgment? Kissing can be like putting a foot on the gas pedal of a car parked on a hill—once you start rolling, it can be hard to hit the brakes.

Scripture Anchor:
"Can a man scoop fire into his lap without his clothes being burned?" (Proverbs 6:27)

Boundaries in Courtship
Why Fences Matter

You ever been to the Grand Canyon? Not the postcard, not the screensaver, but the real thing. It's breathtaking. Wide as forever, deep as mystery, and beautiful enough to stop your heart for a second. But you know what else it is? Dangerous. That's why, all along the edge of those cliffs, they built fences. Not because they're trying to ruin your view—but because they're trying to save your life.

That's what boundaries are like in a God-honoring relationship. They're not about restriction; they're about protection. About giving you space to enjoy the view without falling over the edge.

141

People don't fall off the cliff in one giant leap. It's a toe over the line. Leaning in a little too far. One kiss becomes longer, the hand moves, the heart races, and before you know it, you're dangling off of a ledge God never meant you to dangle from. Not because you're evil—but because you're human. And human emotions—especially the intimate ones—are very powerful. Boundaries keep them safe and keep you from entering a dangerous situation.

Here's the truth: kissing is intimate. It does awaken desire. And it's meant to. God designed it that way—on purpose—for marriage. So, when we treat it like a harmless "hello," we're pretending the canyon isn't there. We're leaning over the railing saying, "I'm just looking." But your heart? It doesn't just look. It feels.

Examples of Boundaries That Protect:

- *No kissing until engagement or marriage. Keeps things simple and hearts focused.*
- *Kissing only in public places. Less temptation, more accountability.*
- *No lying down together—couch, bed, or floor. Horizontal leads to hormonal.*
- *Never being alone in a bedroom. Doors closed = trouble... Actually, maybe just stay out of the bedroom altogether.*
- *Touch limited to holding hands or a quick hug. Keeps affection from turning into arousal.*

God gives us the freedom to build fences—but He also gives us wisdom to know where to place them. And here's a wild thought: boundaries aren't just about what you can handle—they're about protecting the other person's heart too.

Scripture Anchor:
"It is God's will that you should be sanctified: that you should avoid sexual immorality; that each of you should learn to control your own body in a way that is holy and honorable, not in passionate lust like the pagans, who do not know God." (1 Thessalonians 4:3-5)

Points to Ponder

Before you decide where kissing fits in your love story, consider these questions:

- Does this honor The King? Will this act glorify God and reflect His love?

- Does this protect my heart? Am I guarding my emotions and physical desires?

- Does this honor my future spouse? Will I look back on this choice with peace and gratitude?

- Does this align with my boundaries? Am I staying true to the values I've set for myself?

- Am I inviting The King into this decision? Have I prayed for wisdom and guidance?

Let's Bring It In

Princess, The King's desire is for you to walk in freedom, purity, and joy. Physical affection is a gift, but it's also a responsibility. By setting boundaries and seeking His wisdom, you're choosing to honor Him, protect your heart, and prepare for a love story that's truly worth the wait.

So, is it okay to kiss before marriage? That's between you and The King. Just remember: your heart is a treasure, your body is a temple, and your love story is one He's writing with great care. Trust Him, Princess. He knows what's best for you.

A Princess's Vow of Purity

I am a daughter of The King—set apart, chosen, and deeply loved.
My worth is not defined by the world, the attention it gives me, or the
affection of the people in it.

It is defined by the One who made me and gave His life to save me.
Today, I make this vow before my Father, my Savior, and the precious gift
of The Holy Spirit, who lives in me to help me walk righteously.

I will honor God with my body, my thoughts, and my heart. I will not
flippantly give away what was meant to be cherished and valued.
I will wait for intimacy—not out of fear or shame, but because I trust God
to open that door at the right time. Because purity is not a burden—it's an
honor.

I choose to walk out that honor with the wisdom of The Holy Spirit.
He will be my strength when I'm weak, my reminder when I forget, and my
comfort when I feel alone. I will guard my heart and set boundaries.

And if I fall, I won't run *from* God—I will run *to* Him.
His grace will cover me, and His mercy will restore me.

I'm not waiting for a fairytale—I'm walking in His purpose. So, when love
comes, it will find me in Him.

This is my vow—before my Father, my Savior, and His precious Spirit living
within me. I will walk in purity and wait for the man God has for me.
Amen.

9
Emotions

Some days, it feels like there's a tiny, fire-breathing dragon living inside you.

One minute you're laughing, the next you're crying, and ten seconds later, you're mad at your toothbrush. Hormones, right? But here's the secret: your emotions don't have to control you. They're like waves—powerful, overwhelming, but temporary. The King gave you emotions to help you navigate life, but He never meant for them to steer the ship.

When you're feeling all the feels, pause. Pray. Ask The Helper to give you peace. You're not alone in this—The King's got you. So, identify whatever you're feeling—anger, sadness, frustration or that indescribable feeling that drives you crazy—and bring it to your Father in Heaven. He is the best listener, and He won't judge you for having feelings.

Anger: The Fire Within

It starts with a small fire in the trashcan. You barely notice it at first—just a flicker of frustration. But before you know it, the flames have jumped to the curtains, and now they're making their way up the walls.

Panicked, you grab the nearest thing to put it out—a throw pillow—and start frantically smacking the flames. For a moment, it feels like you're making progress, but then you hear it: CRACKLE... WOOSH. The fire has spread to the couch.

Now you're running back and forth, patting out one fire only to see another ignite somewhere else. The harder you try, the faster it spreads—and your house (your life) is quickly turning into a smoky, chaotic mess. By the time the flames finally die out, everything around you is destroyed.

You look around, expecting to find The Dragon hiding behind something—after all, what else could cause this kind of damage? But when the smoke clears, there's only you.

Anger works the same way. It feels small at first—a flicker you think you can control. But left unchecked, it spreads fast, burning through your words, your actions, and even your relationships. The truth is, the biggest battles aren't always against dragons out there—sometimes, it's the storm inside here (pointing to your heart). That's why God calls us to hand our anger over to Him, letting His peace be the water that puts out the flames before they destroy what we love.

> *Let's break it down, shall we?*

Understanding the Damage
Some Things Are Not Replaceable

When anger burns out of control, it doesn't just scorch the surface—it can destroy things that are irreplaceable. Relationships, once warm and inviting, can be reduced to ashes by a few thoughtless words. Opportunities that once felt within reach can vanish in the smoke of a rash decision. Even your own sense of peace can feel suffocated by the haze of regret and bitterness.

Not everything damaged by anger can be rebuilt exactly as it was. Some friendships may never return to their former closeness. Some opportunities may never reopen. But even in the face of loss, The King is a master renovator. While He may not always restore things to their original state, He can create something new—something stronger, something wiser ... *someone* with more self-control. Trusting Him to guide you through the ruins of what's been burned is the first step toward healing.

Scripture Anchor:

"Everyone should be quick to listen, slow to speak and slow to become angry, because human anger does not produce the righteousness that God desires." (James 1:19-20)

Sparks + Accelerant = Disaster

A spark on its own is small and fleeting. Left alone, it might burn out harmlessly. But when you add accelerant—those deeper emotions, unchecked frustrations, or lingering resentments—that tiny spark becomes a raging firestorm. It's the difference between a match lighting a candle and that same match lighting a room soaked in gasoline.

Think about how quickly this happens: your younger sibling borrows your favorite hoodie without asking (spark), and it catches on the accelerant of feeling like no one respects your stuff. Or you scroll through social media and see your friends hanging out without you (spark), which ignites the accelerant of always feeling left out or unwanted.

Maybe you bombed a math quiz, and the spark of disappointment meets the accelerant of pressure to succeed. Before you know it, you're snapping at your parents for asking a simple question or slamming your door for no reason.

The fire spreads faster than you expect, jumping from one emotion to the next, until you're left staring at the damage thinking, "How did it get this bad?" You can't always stop the spark—it catches when you least expect it—but you can deal with the accelerants lying around. Bitterness, insecurity, frustration—those are what make the blaze unstoppable. When you let God clear out what fuels the fire, you can stop destruction before it starts.

Scripture Anchor:
"Fools give full vent to their rage, but the wise bring calm in the end." (Proverbs 29:11)

Call In The Firefighters
The King's Tools to Quench the Flames

Trying to calm your anger by bottling it up or yelling it out is like trying to put out a fire with a throw pillow—it's bound to end in disaster!

You need the right tools, and thankfully, The King's toolkit is fully stocked.

Prayer

Prayer is your 911 call. It's your direct line to the King. When you pray in the midst of anger, you're not just venting—you're calling for intervention. A simple prayer like, "Father, I'm angry," is the spiritual version of saying, "911—there's danger in my house. Please send help." It's asking your Father to step in, protect you, and guide you through the moment before the damage spreads.

Scripture Anchor:

"And pray in the Spirit on all occasions with all kinds of prayers and requests." (Ephesians 6:18)

Scripture

The Bible is your fire extinguisher, filled with wisdom to counteract anger's destructive power. God's Word reminds you to approach situations with grace rather than escalation. When you ground yourself in the Word, you're equipped to respond thoughtfully instead of impulsively.

Scripture Anchor:

"Your word is a lamp for my feet, a light on my path." (Psalm 119:10)

Repentance

This is the blueprint for rebuilding. If the fire has already caused damage, don't leave the room in ruins. Apologize. Seek forgiveness. Take intentional steps to rebuild relationships and repair trust. The King walks with you every step of the way, turning ashes into beauty and scars into stories of redemption.

Scripture Anchor:

"Though I have fallen, I will rise. Though I sit in darkness, the Lord will be my light." (Micah 7:8)

Points to Ponder

- What accelerants are fueling your anger? Take time to identify deeper emotions, like hurt or fear, that may be feeding the flames.

- What sparks are you ignoring? Reflect on moments when anger starts small and think about how you can address it before it grows.

- Are you using the right tools? Consider whether you've been relying on prayer, scripture, and restoration to manage your anger effectively.

- What does rebuilding look like? Ask yourself how you can work with The King to restore what's been lost or create something new in its place.

- How can you prevent future fires? Think about strategies to respond with grace when anger sparks again.

Let's Bring It In

Anger may start as a spark, but it doesn't have to burn down your house. By identifying what fuels your anger, recognizing the damage it can cause, and relying on The King's tools to put out the flames, you can keep your house—the relationships, opportunities, and dreams in your life—safe and whole. Your house is too precious to let anger destroy it, and The King is always ready to help you turn the ashes into beauty.

Conquering Fear and Anxiety

Picture this: your brain has turned into a chaotic detective's basement, complete with a dim light swinging overhead, a corkboard covered in photos, and red yarn crisscrossing in wild, nonsensical patterns. The board is plastered with random snapshots from your life—like the time you forgot someone's name, or when you tripped in front of your class —and anxiety is frantically connecting them all.

In the middle of this tangled mess, a bold headline is scribbled in marker: "BREAKING: You're Going to Fail!" Another note claims, "EXPOSED: Everyone Secretly Thinks You're Awkward!" The connections make no sense, but the longer you stare, the more convincing it feels. That's what anxiety does—it spins wild conspiracy theories about your life, taking small moments and twisting them into catastrophic predictions.

But here's the truth: anxiety's theories are nothing but fiction. The King has already written the real story about you, and it's one of hope, peace, and strength. You don't have to stay stuck in the basement of your thoughts. Let's unpack the lies, expose the truth, and walk into the light.

Let's break it down, shall we?

Exposing Anxiety
The Tabloid Columnist in Your Head

If anxiety had a day job, it would definitely be a tabloid columnist. You know the type—sensational headlines, exaggerated claims, and zero accountability for the chaos they create. It digs through the tiniest details of your life, slaps them onto the front page, and spins stories that would make even the most dramatic soap opera blush.

- Missed a deadline? "SCANDAL: Princess Fails Her Royal Duties!"
- Forgot to text back? "BREAKING: Friendships on the Brink of Ruin!"
- Feeling unprepared? "SHOCKING: She's Totally Out of Her League!"

These headlines are designed to grab your attention and keep you spiraling. They're full of exaggerations and half-truths, but they feel real in the moment.

Anxiety knows how to create drama where none exists, pulling you into a world of doubt and fear. But here's the kicker: none of it is true. Just like you wouldn't let a tabloid define your worth, you don't have to accept anxiety's headlines as fact. The King's story about you is far different. God's Word says you're loved, chosen, and equipped for every challenge you face. Anxiety's rumors are nothing but fake news.

 *Scripture Anchor:*
"For God has not given us a spirit of fear, but of power and of love and of a sound mind." (2 Timothy 1:7)

Community Notes
Fact-Checking Anxiety's Claims

The best way to counter anxiety's conspiracy theories is to challenge them with facts. Start by pausing when the "what-ifs" begin to spiral. Ask yourself, "What's the evidence for this thought?" Then, go to the ultimate source of truth: God's Word.

Here's how you can fact-check anxiety's common lies:

- Lie: "You're not strong enough to handle this."
- Truth: "I can do all things through Christ who strengthens me." (Philippians 4:13)

- Lie: "You're all alone in this struggle."
- Truth: "The Lord Himself goes before you and will be with you; He will never leave you nor forsake you." (Deuteronomy 31:8)

- Lie: "You're not good enough for this opportunity."
- Truth: "For we are God's handiwork, created in Christ Jesus to do good works, which God prepared in advance for us to do." (Ephesians 2:10)

- Lie: "This situation is hopeless."
- Truth: "And we know that in all things God works for the good of those who love Him, who have been called according to His purpose." (Romans 8:28)

- Lie: "You're a failure because you made a mistake."
- Truth: "The Lord upholds all who fall and lifts up all who are bowed down." (Psalm 145:14)

So each time anxiety whispers a lie, cut it down with The King's promises. Anxiety thrives in the absence of clarity, so bringing God's Word into the conversation dismantles its hold. Truth is your greatest weapon.

Prayer

An Exclusive Whistleblowing Interview with The King

Imagine anxiety as a secretive corporation spreading misinformation, planting rumors, and controlling the narrative. Now picture yourself sitting down with the ultimate whistleblower—The King, the Creator, the One who knows everything. That's what prayer is: an exclusive, behind-the-scenes interview with the ultimate source of truth.

When you pray, you're bypassing the noise and going straight to the Father Himself. You're saying, "Here's what I'm hearing, but I need to know the truth." And The King, in His wisdom, responds with clarity and peace:

- "You're not alone—I am with you."
- "You are stronger than you feel right now."
- "I've already written the end of this story, and it's one of victory."

Prayer isn't just a quiet moment of reflection; it's an act of defiance against anxiety's lies. It's shining a light on the rumors, exposing them for what they are, and letting The King's truth take center stage. It's where you exchange fear for faith, doubt for confidence, and chaos for peace.

And here's the beauty: The King never cancels the interview. He's always available, always listening, and always ready to tell you the truth.

FACT-CHECKING ANXIETY
WITH THE BIBLE

Points to Ponder

- Identify the Lies: Anxiety's power lies in its ability to distort the truth. Take time to recognize the falsehoods it tells you.

- Speak God's Truth: Declare Scripture over every anxious thought. The King's promises are stronger than any "what-if."

- Celebrate Small Wins: Each step you take to challenge anxiety—no matter how small—is a victory.

- Lean on Your Community: Share your struggles with trusted friends or mentors who can encourage and support you.

- Stay Present: Anxiety focuses on the future, but peace is found in the here and now.

Let's Bring It In

The grand takeaway? Anxiety may try to run its dramatic headlines and spin wild tales, but The King has already written the real story about you. It's one of love, purpose, and peace. You are not defined by your fears, but by Him. You are a daughter of The King—loved, chosen, and equipped for every challenge.

So take a deep breath, adjust your crown, and step boldly forward. The King is with you, His promises are unshakable, and His peace is stronger than any storm. You've got this—because He's got you.

Deppression Intervention

Do you hear them? Dragging across the floor?
Do you feel them? Pulling tight around your chest?
Depression isn't just another sneaky trick of The Dragon—it's the chains he quietly fastens when you're most tired, most numb, most worn. Unlike anxiety's constant whispers, depression settles in silence. It wraps around your heart and mind until you feel too heavy to move and too foggy to hope It drags you down and tells you to believe that The Kingdom's light is too far... and that The King has forgotten you.

But here's the truth: The King sees you. He hasn't left—and He never will.

Those chains? They're not as strong as they pretend to be. You have the tools to break them. But listen closely: you also have to stop feeding them. The King is right here, ready to help. Prayer, His Word, and praise aren't just survival—they're your escape plan. Your jailbreak. Your freedom song.

Exposing Depression: A Heavy Chain of Lies

Depression is like a set of invisible chains forged from The Dragon's darkest lies. It whispers, "You're not enough," "No one cares," "It's always going to be this way." It wants you to agree. To settle. To sink. But hear me, Princess—every one of those lies is a counterfeit.

The King's truth shatters illusions. He says, "You are fearfully and wonderfully made" (Psalm 139:14). "I will never leave you nor forsake you" (Deuteronomy 31:6). "You are my daughter, and I delight in you" (Zephaniah 3:17). These truths don't just comfort—they break chains.

But breaking chains means you stop feeding the monster. Depression grows when you entertain its lies—when you marinate in sad music, spiral in stuck conversations, and let your thoughts run wild. Don't feed what you're trying to fight.

Breaking Free: The King's Rescue Plan

The Dragon wants to convince you that you're trapped forever. But your Father is a chain-breaker, and freedom is already written into your story.

Call for Reinforcements

You weren't made to fight alone. Your Father, The King, sends allies—pastors, friends, mentors, counselors—because even warriors need backup. Reaching out isn't weakness; it's wisdom.

Scripture Anchor:
"Two are better than one... If either of them falls down, one can help the other up." (Ecclesiastes 4:9–10)

The Word: Your Lock-Breaker

The Dragon lies. The Word tells the truth. When your thoughts say, "You're too broken," the Bible answers, "He heals the brokenhearted" (Psalm 147:3). Every verse is a sword strike, every promise a key in the lock.

Scripture Anchor:
"For the word of God is alive and active. Sharper than any double-edged sword..." (Hebrews 4:12)

Worship Loud, Even When It Hurts

Worship is war. When you sing through your sorrow, you're announcing: *The Dragon doesn't get the last word.* Praise redirects your focus from the weight of the chains to the strength of the Chain-Breaker. Worship is your battle cry.

Scripture Anchor:

"May the praise of God be in their mouths and a double-edged sword in their hands." (Psalm 149:6)

Take Every Thought Captive

You don't have to believe every thought that crosses your mind. Test them. Challenge them. Hold them up to the light of God's Word. If it doesn't line up with the truth, don't let it take root.

Scripture Anchor:

"We demolish arguments and every pretension that sets itself up against the knowledge of God, and we take captive every thought to make it obedient to Christ."
(2 Corinthians 10:5)

Points to Ponder

- When you feel weighed down, what lies does the enemy try to whisper to you? How can you answer with God's truth instead?

- Who in your life can you talk to or pray with when the heaviness feels too heavy to carry alone?

- What scriptures can you keep close to remind you that God is near, even in your darkest moments?

- How can worship, prayer, or journaling help you shift your focus from despair to The King's faithfulness?

- What small step of faith can you take this week to remind yourself that depression doesn't get the final word—God does?

Let's Bring It In

Depression is a heavy chain made of lies from The Dragon, designed to keep you bound in silence and hopelessness. But those chains can be broken. You don't have to stay stuck. Through prayer, God's Word, worship, and trusted allies, you can fight back—and win. But here's the key: you must stop feeding the monster. Don't agree with the lies, dwell in the sadness, or fuel it with things that keep you stuck. Freedom starts when you choose truth over feelings and take every thought captive.

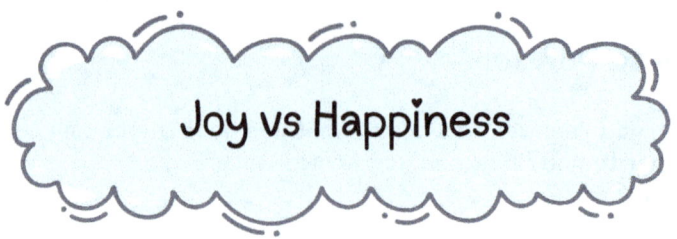

Joy vs Happiness

Happiness is like a balloon—it floats when things go right, but one pop and it's gone. Joy, though? Joy is the light that keeps shining even when the room goes dark. Too many of us chase happiness thinking it'll satisfy, but it's joy—real, biblical joy—that endures when life gets crazy.

> *Let's break it down, shall we?*

Happiness Is a Feeling—Joy Is a Foundation

Happiness depends on what's happening. You ace the test? Happy. Get that new outfit? Happy. Someone compliments you? Happy. But let the day turn, the plan fall apart, the friend stop texting back—and that happiness? It vanishes faster than a text bubble disappearing mid-type.

Joy is different. It's not tied to your circumstances—it's rooted in who your God is. Joy says, "Even if I don't feel good, God is still good." It's the fruit of The Spirit (Galatians 5:22), not the fruit of everything going right. That means it's always available—especially when things go wrong.

 *Scripture Anchor:*
"You make known to me the path of life; you will fill me with joy in your presence..." (Psalm 16:11)

164

Joy Stays When the Storm Stays

When life is hard, people say, "Just be happy." But God says something deeper: "Rejoice in the Lord always." (Philippians 4:4) Not "rejoice in your pain," but rejoice in Him. Why? Because He doesn't change. His presence brings a joy that survives the storm, the silence, and even the sorrow.

Joy doesn't deny pain—it defies it. Joy is choosing to trust, praise, and hope in the middle of the mess. It doesn't mean you're always smiling, but it does mean your spirit doesn't sink with every wave. It's not fake positivity—it's real power rooted in God's presence.

Scripture Anchor:
"Rejoice in the Lord always. I will say it again: Rejoice!"
(Philippians 4:4)

Points to Ponder

- Am I chasing happiness or building my life on joy?

- What's one thing that's been robbing me of joy lately?

- Have I been treating joy like a mood—or a weapon?

- How can I lean into God's presence when I don't feel joyful?

- What would it look like to rejoice in the Lord right now—even in this?

Let's Bring It In

Happiness is nice, but it's fragile. Joy is holy, deep, and indestructible. It comes from the Lord, not the world—and because of that, it lasts. When you stop chasing temporary highs and start living rooted in God's unchanging love, you discover a joy that sings even in the shadows. Don't settle for surface-level happy. Reach for joy. That's where your strength is.

Boredom: When You're Stuck in the Wasteland

Boredom in Dystopia isn't like boredom in the old fairy tales. It's not lounging in a castle waiting for something interesting to happen. It's sitting in the same gray wasteland day after day, staring at the horizon and wondering if The Way Road is ever going to take you somewhere new. The world feels bleak, the journey feels monotonous, and your motivation to keep walking feels nonexistent.

But here's the truth, Princess: boredom isn't a dead end. It's a pause, a space where The King is working behind the scenes—even when it doesn't feel like it. So, before you decide to drop your sword and camp out in the wasteland forever, let's figure out what this season of waiting is trying to teach you.

Let's break it down, shall we?

Boredom as the Quiet Before the Quest

Boredom isn't the enemy—it's the quiet before the next big chapter in your story. It's that strange in-between moment when nothing exciting seems to be happening, but everything is subtly shifting. Think of it as the intermission in a grand play—the lights dim, the stage resets, and everyone wonders what's coming next. That's where you are right now: in the pause before the next scene.

Instead of resenting the stillness, what if you embraced it? This is the space where The King refines you, teaches you to listen, and helps you notice the details you might otherwise miss. The wasteland might not feel exciting, but it's part of The Way Road—a place of preparation, not punishment.

Scripture Anchor:
"See, I am doing a new thing! Now it springs up; do you not perceive it? I am making a way in the wilderness..."
(Isaiah 43:19)

The Wasteland as a Workshop

While boredom whispers that you're stuck, the truth is, this quiet time can be one of the most productive parts of your journey—just not in the flashy, social media way you're used to. Think of the wasteland as a workshop. It's where you get to practice being faithful with the small things: taking care of what's in front of you, honing your talents, and learning how to find joy in the ordinary.

This is also the perfect space to get creative. Ever wonder if you're secretly good at painting, writing, or learning a cool craft like crocheting? Well... now's your chance to find out!

The King loves to see you explore the gifts He's given you, even if they seem small or silly. After all, some of the most unexpected skills end up being the ones He uses for His biggest plans

Scripture Anchor:
"Do not despise these small beginnings, for the Lord rejoices to see the work begin..." (Zechariah 4:10)

Points to Ponder

- The Wasteland Isn't he End: Boredom makes you feel like you're stuck, but The Way Road always leads somewhere. Trust that The King knows where He's taking you—even if the journey feels slow right now.

- Use What You Have: In the wasteland, you might not have much, but The King has given you something. Maybe it's time to pick up that journal, start that project, or reach out to a friend. Small actions lead to big growth.

- Look for Hidden Beauty: Even in the gray wasteland, there are moments of light. A kind word, a sunrise, or a moment of peace—don't overlook the small gifts The King places in your path.

- Ask The King for Perspective: When boredom makes you feel lost, ask The King, "What do You want me to learn here?" His plans are never wasted, and neither is this season.

- Keep Walking: The wasteland feels endless, but it's not. Keep putting one foot in front of the other, trusting that The King will guide you out of this season in His perfect time.

Let's Bring It In

Princess, the wasteland of boredom might feel bleak, but it's not where your story ends. It's just a chapter—a pause for growth, reflection, and preparation. The King hasn't forgotten about you, and The Way Road hasn't disappeared. He's working in the stillness, shaping you for what's ahead.

So, don't give up. Keep walking, keep trusting, and keep looking for the beauty in the ordinary. The wasteland is just a season, and The King is leading you to something greater.

10
Facing Hard Trials

You didn't choose these trails. They showed up uninvited, unwelcome, and unfair.

Some roads show up uninvited—grief, sickness, betrayal, loss. Maybe you've watched a friend walk away, or watched someone you love suffer not knowing how to help. Maybe you're the one suffering, or maybe you are the one left behind after the funeral. These are the trails that test your faith and shake your heart.

I'm not going to sugarcoat the pain—but I am here to remind you that you're not walking through it alone. The King is with you in the questions, in the ache, in the silence. And even here, He's still writing redemption into your story.

Let's Pause a Moment to Talk About... Biscuits

Ingredients
Flour. Baking soda. Salt. Buttermilk.
And a stick of butter.

If you were to taste any of those ingredients on their own, you'd probably gag. Dry. Bitter. Sour. Overwhelming. Not one of them tastes "good." Not even close. But when a baker steps in and starts mixing, kneading, rolling—and then slides that messy blob into the fire—something starts to change. What was once a bunch of gross ingredients becomes golden, soft, warm biscuits.

Your life might feel like that right now—like you're chewing on a mouthful of baking soda. A breakup. A betrayal. A diagnosis. A closed door. By itself, it's bitter. But God's not serving that moment as the whole meal. He's still mixing it. Working it together. Turning up the heat in order to bake something better.

And that's not even the best news. The *best* news is that this isn't just an ordinary cook we're talking about... Your Father is the Master Chef. And He knows exactly how much of each hard thing to use. Nothing in your life is wasted—not the tears, not the delays, not the confusion. They're all going into the recipe. And one day, when the timer dings, you'll look back and say, "Oh. That's why that happened." And it'll taste like peace. Like purpose. Like delicious biscuits fresh out the oven.

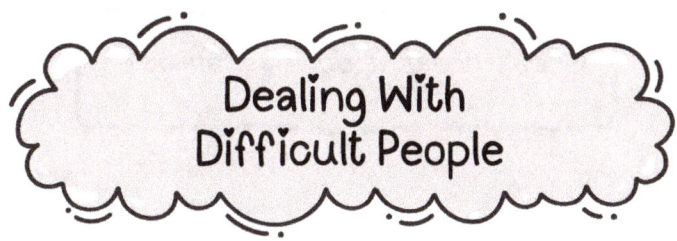

Dealing With Difficult People

Wouldn't life be a dream if everyone treated you like the royalty you are? But here's the truth, Princess, not everyone is going to bow to your kindness or cheer for your victories. Some people are just... difficult. And let's not sugarcoat it—some are downright mean. And then there are those people who know how to test your last nerve!

But whether they're stomping on your vibe, throwing shade at your sparkle, or simply refusing to let you live in peace, unfortunately these encounters are... inevitable.

But guess what? You're not navigating this royal road alone. The King has equipped you with everything you need to handle even the most challenging people in this crazy world. So grab your crown and let's figure out how to keep your grace intact while dealing with difficult, mean, and annoying people.

> *Let's break it down, shall we?*

When Someone's Just...Really Annoying

Some people are just... a lot. Maybe they interrupt every sentence, chew too loud, or act like the world revolves around them and their playlist. But annoying doesn't always mean bad—it might just mean different. The King calls you to patience, not perfection. That doesn't mean you have to fake a smile or pretend it doesn't bother you. It just means choosing grace over grumbling—and remembering you've probably been that person before, too.

Still, patience doesn't mean you have to be besties. It's okay to set space and boundaries. But when you do interact, ask The King to help you see beyond the irritation. Sometimes, the ones who bug you most are the ones who need kindness most. And if they're just being extra for no reason? Smile, breathe, and hand it to The King.

Scripture Anchor:
"Put on then, as God's chosen ones, holy and beloved, compassionate hearts, kindness, humility, meekness, and patience," (Colossians 3:12)

174

Dealing with Difficult Authority

When someone in authority—like a teacher, coach, or boss —is being difficult or unkind, it's tough. You might feel upset or even powerless. But as a daughter of The King, you're still called to show respect and humility, even when it's hard. That doesn't mean pretending it's okay or letting someone mistreat you—it means handling it with grace and wisdom.

Part of growing with God is learning to hold your tongue when you want to snap back. It means still doing your duties well... even when the person giving the instructions is being a big meanie-head.

However, if someone in charge crosses a serious line, you should never stay silent. Talk to your parents or a trusted adult who can help you process what's happening. God cares deeply about your heart and your safety. Showing respect doesn't mean ignoring what's wrong—it means trusting The King to guide your response with courage, truth, and love.

Scripture Anchor:
"Likewise, you who are younger, be subject to the elders. Clothe yourselves, all of you, with humility toward one another, for 'God opposes the proud but gives grace to the humble." (1 Peter 5:5)

But God... What about the Really Mean Ones

You know the ones. The people who don't just annoy you—they wound you. The ones who make it personal. Who lie, exclude, mock, or manipulate. The ones who leave you wondering, *How can someone be this cruel and still sleep at night?*

Here's the truth: God sees them too. He saw every insult. Every backstab. Every time they made you question your worth. And while *you* might feel powerless to stop them...

He is not.

You're not crazy for hurting. You're not weak for feeling it. And forgiveness doesn't mean pretending it didn't matter. Forgiveness means refusing to carry what only The King can.

Princess, The King sees what's happening here. And He will work this out. He has His own way of making it right. And while He's working in the background, you have an opportunity to use wisdom and...
set some BOUNDARIES.

Boundaries... They aren't walls to keep people out. They're actually fences to protect what's sacred. Setting limits doesn't make you unkind—it makes you wise. The King calls you to love others, but not at the expense of your peace or dignity. Boundaries say, "I can love you, but I won't let you hurt me."

Here's what that might look like:
- "I forgive you, but I'm not going to hang out or talk to you unless an adult is present—for accountability."
- "I'm happy to help sometimes, but I can't keep saying yes when it drains me. I need peace in my life too."
- "I forgive you, but I need a time out. This dynamic isn't healthy for either of us. So, I'm giving this relationship to God and trusting Him to heal what we can't fix right now."

Remember, The King isn't asking you to stay where you're being torn apart. He's asking you to walk in truth—and sometimes, that means walking away.

BUT...

Here's the holy plot twist: you can also HEAL.
Because "But God" changes everything.
- They meant to tear you down — *BUT GOD* is building something stronger in you.
- They wanted to leave you bitter — *BUT GOD* is rooting you in grace.
- They thought they had the last word — *BUT GOD* never stopped writing your story.

So what about the really mean ones?
Let The King handle them.
Your job is to heal. To grow. To walk in peace while
He deals with the rest.

Scripture Anchor:

"Do not take revenge... but leave room for God's wrath, for it is written: 'It is mine to avenge; I will repay,' says the Lord." (Romans 12:19)

Scripture Anchor:

"But I say to you, Love your enemies and pray for those who persecute you." (Matthew 5:44)

Forgiveness Doesn't Mean Being a Doormat

Forgiveness is not the same thing as permission. You can forgive someone and still walk away. You can let go of your anger without giving them permission to keep hurting you.

Forgiveness is about *your* freedom. It's about laying down the weight of bitterness at the feet of the only One qualified to judge.

Because The King will bring justice. He saw the moment they crossed the line. And He cares deeply about how it made you feel. Your job isn't to carry the offense. Your job is to place it in *His* hands, trust *Him* to take care of it and FORGIVE.

Scripture Anchor:

"For if you forgive others their trespasses, your heavenly Father will also forgive you, but if you do not forgive others their trespasses, neither will your Father forgive your trespasses." (Matthew 6:14-15)

Why Does The King Let This Happen?

It's a fair question, Princess. Why does The King allow these thorny people in our lives? The answer: they're part of your royal training. Dealing with them builds your patience, strengthens your faith, and shapes your character. Every time you choose grace over frustration, you're becoming more like The King Himself.

Scripture Anchor:
"Not only that, but we rejoice in our sufferings, knowing that suffering produces endurance, and endurance produces character, and character produces hope." (Romans 5:3-4)

Points to ponder

- Have I paused to ask The King for wisdom before reacting, or am I just firing back out of frustration?

- Is my response showing kindness and strength, or just trying to win the moment?

- Am I setting boundaries with love, or building walls out of bitterness?

- Have I prayed for this person? Or have I just vented about them?

- What do I need to release to The King instead of carrying it on my own?

Let's Bring It In

Princess, difficult, mean, and annoying people are not your enemies. They're part of The Dragon's scheme to trip you up, but they're also part of The King's plan to refine you. You have the power to rise above their negativity and shine with His light.

When someone tests your patience, remember who you are: a daughter of The King, equipped with grace, strength, and the ability to love even when it's hard. And when in doubt? Pray. The King hears you, strengthens you, and fights for you. So wear your crown high, hold your peace, and let The King handle the rest.

Losing Friends
When Your Court Changes

Friendship breakups hit differently, don't they? It's not like an argument with a sibling or losing a favorite sweater—it's losing a piece of your heart. One moment, they're your partner-in-crime, the one who knows all your quirks, and the next? They're gone. Maybe they drifted away, maybe there was a fallout, or maybe life just pulled you in different directions. Whatever the cause, the emptiness stings, and you're left staring at an empty space in your life, wondering if it will ever feel full again.

But Princess, here's the thing: even when your court feels empty, your Father, The King, has a plan. The empty seats at your table? He's already preparing the right people to fill them. And in the meantime, He's right there with you, helping you navigate the ache.

When Seasons Shift, Friendships Do Too

Friendships, like seasons, change. It's a truth that's hard to accept but important to understand. Some friendships are meant for a lifetime, while others are just for a season.

It doesn't make the time you shared less valuable. It doesn't mean you or your friend failed. It just means that your paths have taken different directions. And sometimes, that's okay. Ecclesiastes 3:1 reminds us, "There is a time for everything, and a season for every activity under the heavens." That includes relationships.

Scripture Anchor:
"For I am about to do something new. See, I have already begun! Do you not see it?" (Isaiah 43:19)

The Dragon's Lies in the Transition

As soon as the furniture is gone and the room feels empty, The Dragon loves to sneak in and whisper his lies again:

- "See? You're all alone now." *Not true.* The King never leaves you alone, and He's already planning to fill your court with new relationships.

- "You'll never find better friends." *Lies.* The King's design is always better than what came before. He knows exactly what you need in this season of your life.

- "This is your fault." *Wrong again.* Friendships change for many reasons, and sometimes you can't control it.

Scripture Anchor:
"Put on the full armor of God, so that you will be able to stand firm against the schemes of the devil." (Ephesians 6:11)

Trusting The King's Design

Here's the hope, Princess: your court won't stay empty forever. The King is working behind the scenes, preparing new friendships that fit the shape of your story—friends who will walk with you, sharpen you, and encourage you.

But if you've lost friends lately, let's name that ache. Maybe they left without warning. Maybe you pushed them away. Maybe it blew up. Or maybe you just grew apart over time. Some friendships break because of hurt. Some just shift with life. Others drift for reasons you'll never fully understand.

Still, the silence feels heavy. But hear this: you haven't been abandoned. You've been invited into renovation.

God is remodeling your heart—not because you failed, but because He's making space. He's teaching you to trust again, to heal, to grow. He's teaching you to not base your identity in who walked away—but to anchor your life in the One who never will. And when the work is done? The doors will open. The room will glow. And the right people will take their seats—right on time, and right on purpose.

Scripture Anchor:
"...He will give a crown of beauty for ashes, a joyous blessing instead of mourning, festive praise instead of despair..."
(Isaiah 61:3)

Points to Ponder

Your Father doesn't leave empty spaces empty forever. He's not just renovating your court for the sake of change—He's designing it to match the new season of your life.

- **Healing Comes First:** Let The King tend to your heart. Sit with Him in prayer, pour out your hurt, and let His love fill the cracks. Psalm 147:3 promises, "He heals the brokenhearted and binds up their wounds."

- **Growth Through Loss:** The King uses every loss to teach and shape you. Maybe He's teaching you to trust Him more, showing you how to set healthy boundaries, or preparing you for deeper, more meaningful friendships in the future.

- **New Connections Will Come:** Trust The King's timing. He's already preparing new friends who will walk with you in this season, bringing encouragement, joy, and growth.

Let's Bring It In

Losing friends feels unsettling, lonely, and makes you wonder if it'll ever feel right again. But Princess, The King isn't finished. He's clearing the space to bring in something better—new friendships that fit this season of your life perfectly.

In the meantime, let Him heal your heart, teach you through the loss, and remind you that your worth isn't tied to who stays or goes.

Greif and Loss

These are moments for tissues, tears, and working through tough emotions. I know you may not want to go there, but we're all going to have to face this issue eventually. That's right. I'm talking about Grief and Loss. This is the kind of pain that makes it hard to breathe, like someone ripped the colors from your world and left you with nothing but gray.

Maybe it's losing a grandparent who felt like your anchor, a beloved pet who was your constant companion, or something too big for words—like losing someone you thought would always be there. In these moments, The Dragon loves to sneak in with his cruel whispers: "Your Father doesn't care. If He did, why would this happen? And that White Knight? He couldn't have defeated death. Because if He did, this wouldn't hurt so much."

These are lies sraight from the Devil.

But let's be honest, grief can make lies sound louder than truth, can't it? It can shake your faith, make you question your Father's love, even blur the glory of The White Knight. But hear this: your Father's love has never faltered, The Helper still breathes comfort into your storm, and Jesus hasn't just won the victory—He is the Victory. No darkness, no grave, no grief can undo what He's already finished

> ## Let's break it down, shall we?

The White Knight:
He Knows and He Paid for This Pain

Let's talk about Jesus, The White Knight, your Champion. Grief isn't foreign to Him. He knows your pain. When He stood at the tomb of His friend Lazarus, He wept—even though He knew He was about to raise him from the dead. Why? Because death, loss, and grief hurt. They aren't part of The Kingdom your Father designed, and Jesus felt the weight of that brokenness deeply.

But here's the even greater truth: Jesus didn't just know pain—He carried it. When He was nailed to that cross, He bore every ounce of grief, heartbreak, and sorrow that you've ever felt.

When He stretched out His arms and declared, "It is finished," He wasn't only defeating sin—He was carrying your pain, breaking its power, and building a bridge from sorrow to salvation. And because of that victory, this grief—no matter how suffocating—will not last forever. The empty tomb stands as proof: death doesn't get the final word. Jesus does.

Scripture Anchor:
"He himself bore our sins in his body on the cross, so that we might die to sins and live for righteousness; by his wounds you have been healed." (1 Peter 2:24)

Your Father in Heaven
The Redemption Bringer

Here's the thing: your grief didn't catch your Father off guard. He's not scrambling to figure out what to do or panicking about how to fix it. No—He saw this moment coming before you were even born, and He's been weaving His plan of redemption into your story all along.

This doesn't mean He waves a magic wand and erases your grief. Instead, He takes the broken pieces of your heart and creates something new—something more beautiful than you could have imagined. It's what He does best: taking the ashes of sorrow and turning them into something amazing.

Does this mean your loss was "good"? Of course not. Grief and death were never part of The Kingdom your Father intended. But The King is so good, so powerful, and so loving that He can take even the darkest moments and use them for your good.

But here's the hard part: your Father's plan unfolds on *His* timeline, not yours. Healing may not come as quickly as you'd like, and the beauty He's creating from your pain may take time to appear.

But trust this: your Father is never late. And one day, when the grief fades, you'll look back and see how faithful He has been. You'll see how He carried you, comforted you, and worked—even this pain—together for good.

Scripture Anchor:
"And we know that in all things God works for the good of those who love him, who have been called according to his purpose." (Romans 8:28)

The Helper's Comfort:
I'm The Healer of Your Soul

And then there's me—The Helper, your 24/7 Comforter. When the weight of grief feels unbearable, I am there to carry you. I'm the gentle voice reminding you of The King's promises. The warm presence wrapping around you when you feel cold and alone. The strength that gets you through a day you didn't think you could face.

It may not be the Father's will to always take the pain away instantly, but whatever the situation, my job is to walk with you through it. I will remind you of The White Knight's victory and help you cling to the truth when The Dragon's lies feel overwhelming. I promise.

Scripture Anchor:
"When you pass through the waters, I will be with you; and when you pass through the rivers, they will not sweep over you. When you walk through the fire, you will not be burned; the flames will not set you ablaze." (Isaiah 43:2)

Points to Ponder:

The Dragon's Lies vs. The Truth of The Kingdom

- The Lie: "Your Father doesn't care."
  - The Truth: Your Father's love for you is unshakable. He gave His Son, The White Knight, for you, and He is holding you through this pain.

- The Lie: "The White Knight's sacrifice doesn't matter."
  - The Truth: The cross is proof that Jesus defeated sin, death, and grief itself. His resurrection is your hope that this pain isn't the end of the story.

- The Lie: "You're alone in this."
  - The Truth: The Helper is with you, your Father is near, and you are surrounded by His love. You are never alone.

Let's Bring It In

I know. Grief is heavy, and it's okay to feel the weight of it. It's okay to cry, to question, to ask your Father, "Why?" But don't let The Dragon's lies keep you from the truth.

The White Knight bore this pain for you, and His victory means that grief doesn't get the last word. Because your Father—The King—has a plan, and He is working all of this pain together for your good. And you also have The Helper with you. I will be comforting you along the way and reminding you that you are never alone.

When Health Problems Hit Home

Hey Princess.

I see you. And I don't just mean that in a polite way. No. I mean, I really, really see you. In the hospital rooms, during the late-night blood sugar checks, in the midst of the breathing treatments and bone scans... the pill schedules taped to the fridge, the mirror you avoid on the hard days.

I see you in the quiet moments when your body aches, when your strength slips away without warning, when you lie in bed and whisper, "Why me?" or "Why them?"

I see your courage, your questions, your grit, your grief... and the way you keep going anyway.

In the midst of all that pain... I'm right here. Whispering strength when yours runs out. Holding your hand through it —not just to comfort you, but to carry you when your heart trembles and says, "I can't go on any further."

So let's talk about this—just me and you. Because health problems aren't just some "grown-up" thing. They hit lockers, lunchrooms, bedrooms, and hearts. They show up with names like type 1 diabetes, cystic fibrosis, Crohn's, muscular dystrophy, cerebral palsy, epilepsy, childhood cancer... or sometimes there's no name at all—just questions the doctors can't answer yet.

Whatever the hardship, when it hits your life personally, it can feel like the purpose and light of living have flickered out. But I promise you, Princess, even here—in this painful place—the journey isn't over. It's just beginning.

> *Let's break it down, shall we?*

Pain & Suffering
When Your Body Feels Broken

Some girls dream of dances, recitals, or soccer games. And some... some just dream of making it through the day without their body turning into a battlefield.

Maybe your pancreas checked out early. Maybe your lungs don't work like everyone else's. Maybe your diagnosis has a name you had to Google five times just to pronounce.

Whatever your situation, let me say this plainly: you are not your diagnosis. You are not weak. And you are definitely not a burden. Your body just needs a little extra help.

Most people don't understand the kind of bravery you show just by waking up and trying again.
But I do. And guess what? I don't just visit you on your strong days. I dwell with you in the middle of the mess.

Every injection, every round of treatment, every "no" when you wanted to say "yes," is another chance to lean into the supernatural strength I'm pouring into you. And remember, Princess—your body may falter, but your God never will.

When You're Okay
But Someone You Love Is Suffereing

Sometimes it's not your own body that breaks—it's your mom's, your brother's, or someone you love so deeply that it aches just to breathe. Maybe you've watched a parent fight cancer or held your sibling's hand through another long hospital night.

Let's be honest—it can feel helpless. Watching someone you love suffer can make you feel like your prayers are hitting the ceiling, like hope packed its bags and left for good.

But sweet girl, do not underestimate your presence in this story.

Your love, your prayers, your tears, your "I'm here for you"—that's holy ground stuff. You carry God's peace when you walk into the room. You give His grace when you lend your strength as theirs begins to fade. You become your Father's voice when you whisper, "It's okay to cry." You don't have to fix what's broken—you never did. But oh, how God uses you to comfort the brokenhearted.

The Secret About Suffereing
It's Like a Superpower... It Makes You Stronger

Nobody signs up for suffering. It's the worst. But listen—it's also where the power gets real. Suffering presses you closer to God. It strips away the glittery distractions and reveals what truly matters. And here's the miracle: the very pain that tried to break you becomes the place where your Father rebuilds you—not in spite of the suffering, but through it.

And in that place, you find something sacred—the fellowship of suffering. It's where you begin to understand Jesus in a way you never could from a distance.

The One who bled, wept, and carried the sorrow of the world now sits beside you in yours. And as you begin to see His wounds, somehow, the ones in your heart begin to heal.

Spoiler Alert
One Day, the Pain Ends—And True Life Begins

Because I know what you've been through—the long nights, the surgeries, the IV drips, and the anxiety that comes with each test result. I see the tears that hit your pillow after everyone else has fallen asleep. I feel the weight of this burden and how it presses against your life. And I cradle the flicker of hope your heart keeps whispering... that someday—somehow—it will all get better.

Princess, hold on to that hope. Because it's real, and it speaks truth.

One day, all this pain, all this sickness, every broken cell, every bruised heart—will be over. Not because *you* were strong enough to push through, but because *He* was. The White Knight. The One who took every sickness, every sorrow, every wound—and carried it on a wooden cross so you could come Home.

This world? It's not the end of the story—it's just the first chapter. And when you choose to come back to the Father, walking the road Jesus paved with His own blood, you're saying yes to a future where healing isn't just a hope—it's a promise.

No more needles. No more pills.
No more monitors or oxygen tanks or hospital bracelets.
No more pain.

Only joy. Only peace. Only dancing. Whole.
Fully-healed. Fully-known. Fully-loved and forever filled with joy in The Kingdom that never hurts.

Your scars? They'll become stories of victory.
Your tears? He'll wipe every last one away.
And your heart? It'll finally be at rest.
Forever.

Scriptures to Read
During Times of Suffering

2 Corinthians 12:9

"My grace is sufficient, for my power is made perfect in weakness.' Therefore I will boast all the more gladly about my weaknesses, so that Christ's power may rest on me."

Isaiah 41:10

"So do not fear, for I am with you; do not be dismayed, for I am your God. I will strengthen you and help you; I will uphold you with my righteous right hand."

Psalm 34:18

"The Lord is close to the brokenhearted and saves those who are crushed in spirit."

Romans 8:18

"I consider that our present sufferings are not worth comparing with the glory that will be revealed in us."

Matthew 11:28

"Come to me, all you who are weary and burdened, and I will give you rest."

Revelation 21:4

"He will wipe every tear from their eyes. There will be no more death or mourning or crying or pain, for the old order of things has passed away."

Points to Ponder

- How has this struggle (or my loved one's) taught me to lean on God's strength instead of my own? What can others learn from my perseverance?

- Am I letting shame or comparison steal my joy because of how my body is different?

- Who around me might need encouragement right now—someone who feels weak or forgotten? (Remember, your pain can actually become someone else's light.)

- How does hope play a part in this struggle?

Let's Bring It In

When health problems hit home, they don't get the final word—God does: your Father in Heaven, your Savior Jesus, and Me (The Helper, a.k.a. The Holy Spirit). And We say: You are loved, not left behind. You are carried, not crushed. Whether the sickness is yours or someone else's, Our presence is steady. Our strength is endless. And together—we'll turn even this into something breathtaking.

You're not walking through this alone, Princess. You have your Father shining down on you, your Savior interceding for you, and Me.
I'm here. Every ache, every test, every tear—I'm already there, holding your heart in My hands. Always.

11
Looking Forward

Every season brings change—new schools, new challenges, new chances to grow.

Maybe you're stepping into middle school, high school, or even college. Maybe you're learning how to walk with God for real this time, not just on Sundays. Whatever's ahead, know this: your story is still in the Master's hands. The King is still leading, still shaping, still walking right beside you.

It's time to focus on moving forward with purpose—becoming who you were made to be and keeping your eyes on the day you'll see your Father face-to-face. Until then, we walk. We grow. We keep going—one step, one season, one promise at a time.

New Class. Same Crown.

So, you're the new kid... again. Whether it's middle school with its weird cafeteria smells and everyone suddenly obsessed with deodorant, high school with its hallway hierarchy and social media chaos, or college where people act like adults but still eat cereal for dinner—starting something new can feel like stepping onto a stage with no script.

But let me tell you this: your identity doesn't get erased just because your schedule changed. You're still royalty. You still belong. The King's got you—even if your first day includes spinach in your teeth, getting your period during gym class or calling your professor "mom" by accident (true story, it happens).

Let's break it down, shall we?

Middle School:
The Start of the Climb

This is where everything starts to shift. Bodies change. Friendships get complicated. School gets harder, and suddenly everyone seems to care way too much about who's cool and who's not. You might feel like you're constantly one wrong move away from total embarrassment. (Spoiler: You're not. Everyone else is way too worried about themselves to be worrying about *your* awkward moments.)

Here's what matters more than your backpack brand or where you sit at lunch: You belong. Not because you fit in perfectly—but because you're already chosen. By God. Your Creator. Your Father.

Middle school isn't about having it all figured out—it's about learning how to hold onto who you are when everything around you starts shifting. It's okay to grow slow. It's okay to feel awkward. But don't forget—your crown isn't something you earn from your peers. It was given by your Father, paid for by your Savior, and kept by the Holy Spirit. You're in good hands, Princess.

Scripture Anchor:
"You are a chosen people. You are royal priests, a holy nation, God's very own possession. As a result, you can show others the goodness of God, for he called you out of the darkness into his wonderful light." (1 Peter 2:9)

High School:
Finding Your Voice

High school isn't one-size-fits-all. Some girls wake up at 6 a.m. to catch a bus. Some roll out of bed and crack open a laptop at home. Some do classes from books at the kitchen table while little siblings run laps in the background. Whether you're in public school, private school, homeschool, or somewhere in between—you're still right in the middle of one of the most shaping seasons of your life.

Here's the thing about high school: it's going to stretch you. Not just academically, but emotionally, spiritually, and socially. This is the season when you start asking deeper questions—Who am I? What do I actually believe? Where do I fit in?

Some days, you'll feel confident. Other days, you'll wonder if you're behind, missing out, or just plain lost. But no matter what your school day looks like, you are not left out of God's plan. Whether you're navigating locker drama or learning Latin with your mom as the teacher—you are still growing into the woman He designed you to be.

High school is where you really begin finding your voice, your convictions and your *tribe*. You'll learn what real friendships look like—and what to do when they fall apart. You'll face temptation, peer pressure, and big decisions. And in the middle of it all, you'll also start seeing your calling come into focus.

This is your time to grow in grit and grace—to learn responsibility, to build habits that stick, and to stand your ground when the world says, "Change to fit in."

Remember, God didn't call you to be popular. He called you to be faithful. And that matters in every part of high school —how you talk, how you work, how you treat people, and how you carry yourself when no one's watching. That's what it means to be a girl for God.

Scripture Anchor:
"...the Lord has told you what is good, and this is what he requires of you: to do what is right, to love mercy, and to walk humbly with your God." (Micah 6:8)

College and the Real World Experience:
Becoming Her

This is the season where the training wheels come off. Whether you're walking into a college classroom or clocking in for your first *real* job—life just got realer. The schedule is yours. The decisions are yours. The responsibility is yours. And so is the growth.

You may be balancing dorm life and class projects with coffee-fueled study nights. Or you may have chosen to head right into the workforce, where you are navigating work shifts, bills, and what it means to show up—even on the days you don't feel like it.

Both paths are valid. Both are valuable. And both are part of becoming *her*—the woman who stands for God with confidence, walks with His wisdom, and carries herself like royalty because she knows who her Father is.

In this season, your faith won't just be something you inherited—it'll be something *you* choose. You'll be tested in ways you weren't before. You'll make decisions that shape your future. You'll learn what real maturity looks like—not just doing what's required, but doing what's right. Not just showing up, but showing who you are when you do.

There's beauty in becoming.

And it doesn't require a certain title, paycheck, or diploma. It requires obedience. Grit. Humility. And a whole lot of grace. The King's not grading you on your major or your job title—He's refining your character, growing your gifts, and teaching you to walk like the daughter He's called you to be.

So wherever you are—study hall, job site, office, or online—know this: you're not falling behind. You're stepping forward. Becoming her. Becoming His.

Scripture Anchor:
"Being confident of this, that he who began a good work in you will carry it on to completion until the day of Christ Jesus." (Philippians 1:6)

Points to Ponder ⭐

- Middle School: Am I trying to change who I am just to fit in— or am I learning to stand tall in who God already says I am?

- High School: Am I letting my peers define me—or am I building my life on truth that doesn't shift with the crowd?

- College: Now that it's up to me, am I making space for God in my schedule—or just squeezing Him in when it's convenient?

- Workforce: Do I treat my job like a stepping stone—or a training ground for character, faith, and leadership?

- All Seasons: No matter where I am, do I believe I'm becoming her—the woman God sees—even if I can't see the full picture yet?

Let's Bring It In

School isn't just about textbooks and tests. Every new grade, every new season, every shift in schedule is shaping you. Whether you're adjusting to middle school chaos, finding your voice in high school, juggling freedom and responsibility in college, or learning real-world lessons on the job—this is your training ground.

You're not just learning facts. You're learning faith. You're discovering how to show up with character, how to carry your crown with confidence, and how to walk with wisdom in unfamiliar places.

So embrace the learning, even when it's messy. God doesn't waste a single season. You're not falling behind. You're growing deeper. You're moving forward. You're becoming her.

Growing with God

You don't grow because you downloaded a five-step plan. You grow because you keep coming back. Because even when you wander, you wander toward your Father, your Savior, and Me. Because you keep whispering "yes" when it would be easier to shut down.

And that? That's the key to growing with God.

Spiritual maturity isn't a trophy. It's a trail. And you're not walking it alone. Every uneven, uphill, tear-streaked step — I'm right there. Your Father sent Me to help you walk it.

But I'm not helping alone. Jesus—your Knight in shining armor—is also interceding for you right now at the Father's throne. Which is wild when you really stop and think about it.

Because it means this:
God sent the Spirit of God to help you get closer to God, while God intercedes before God for you as you walk in the Spirit of God to get closer to God... Mind. Blown.

So if you're growing—even slowly—you're not doing it alone. The Father is drawing you, the Son is praying for you, and I'm right here helping you take the next step.

Let's break it down, shall we?

Feed on the Word
(Your spiritual being needs spiritual food)

The Bible isn't a rulebook. It's a feast. It's not for skimming, flexing, or checking off—it's for breaking open and digging in. Come barefoot and curious. Come with your questions. Come mid-breakdown if you have to. Bring the coffee stains, the honest doubts, the whole mess of you. Because when you open those pages, the Helper—aka the Holy Spirit—is already there.

My job as the Helper is to open your understanding and shine light where you couldn't see before. That conviction in your heart, or the comfort you feel when the words land like they were written for your exact moment—that's God's Spirit working, drawing you closer to your Father and your Savior, Jesus.

So don't rush. Don't scan.
Just settle in and enjoy the feast.

 *Scripture Anchor:*
"Man shall not live on bread alone, but on every word that comes from the mouth of God." (Matthew 4:4)

Stay In Prayer
(Stay online)

Forget formulas. Forget sounding holy. Just talk to your Father. Don't wait until you have the right words—He's not grading your grammar. He's your Dad. And He already knows.

Prayer isn't about performance—it's about presence.
Just show up with an honest heart. The Helper (that's Me) will help you do the rest.

I'm here to pull you in close. I remind you who you're talking to: the One who knit you together and still holds you when you come undone. When you're afraid to approach Him, I give you the boldness. When you don't know what to say, I give you the words—or sit with you in the silence until the tears stop flowing.

Prayer isn't a monologue—it's an exchange.
You speak—I guide.
You listen—I illuminate.
You cry—I carry it straight to His heart.

And when you slow down long enough to breathe, you'll hear your Father speak. His voice isn't always loud. Most days, it comes soft—like a whisper. But when He needs to, that same voice carries the strength of many waters.

Whatever His approach, remember this: God still speaks, Princess.

Are you listening?

Scripture Anchor:
"In the same way, the Spirit helps us in our weakness. We do not know what we ought to pray for, but the Spirit himself intercedes for us through wordless groans." (Romans 8:26)

Growth in the Gathering
(Communion in the Chaos)

You weren't meant to be a one-person revival. Growth thrives in community... real—sometimes awkward—kingdom community.

Yes, they'll rub you the wrong way. They'll frustrate you. And sometimes they'll even hurt your feelings. But they'll also encourage you, pray with you, and show up when you're in need. And when you least expect it, your Father will use them to bless you in ways that will completely surprise you.

Blessing and frustration are both part of the path. God grows you through the tension and the tenderness—just like He did with the disciples.

And just like the disciples, the church is your family. You share the same blood—His. The blood Jesus poured out at Calvary binds you and these people together.

These are the individuals who you will love and share eternity with. So you may as well start practicing being together now.

My point is... don't ghost the gathering. Don't retreat because someone burned you or hurt your feelings. Because when God is done, that same person may be the one who blesses you.

And remember—*I'm* in the gathering too. I'm in that awkward prayer circle and late-night prayer call. I'm in those "Will you forgive me?" moments and the "I feel led to tell you..." encouragements that often show up when the Word of God goes forth. Princess, that's not just church being church... that's God speaking.

Scripture Anchor:
"Let us think of ways to motivate one another to acts of love and good works. And let us not neglect our meeting together, as some people do, but encourage one another..."
(Hebrews 10:24–25)

Points to Ponder

- When I open the Word, am I reading to finish or reading to be changed? What would it look like to feed on it instead of skimming through it?

- Have I made prayer a habit or a heart-to-heart? What's one thing I need to say to the Father that I've been holding back?

- What might God be trying to say to me through the people He's placed in my life—even the difficult ones?

- Am I showing up to the gathering with expectation or hesitation? What would it mean to come not just to receive, but to release what God's put in me?

- Where in my life am I resisting growth because it feels uncomfortable? And where is The Helper nudging me to stay rooted and keep going?

Let's Bring It In

You don't grow because you nailed a spiritual to-do list. You grow because He was nailed to the cross and opened the door. You grow because you keep walking, because you keep talking to Him, and because you keep feeding on every word in Scripture. You grow because you're rooted in community.

So keep opening the page. Keep speaking to Him. Keep leaning into His love—even on the days you don't feel worthy of it. Because He's not waiting at the finish line—He's walking right beside you.

Eternity and Beyond

Okay, Princess. Let's talk about forever. Not the kind of "forever" you say when a class feels too long or a heartbreak drags on. I mean the real kind—the forever your soul was made for. The one that stretches beyond time, beyond space, beyond every breath you've ever taken.
The one where I will still be right here with you.

Eternity isn't a concept. It's a homecoming. And I want you to get excited about it—not afraid or confused. So let Me explain what's ahead, what's promised, and what's waiting just past the veil.

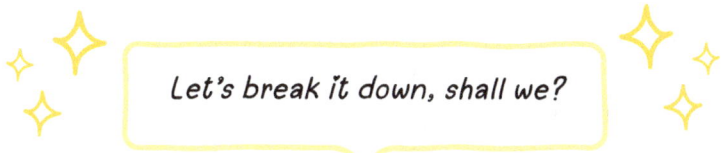

Let's break it down, shall we?

Two Doors, One Promise
(By Death Or His Return)

He said He was coming back for you.
Not just to visit. Not just to wave from a distance.
But to get you. To take you by the hand and bring you Home.
And He wasn't lying.

Whether by the clouds or through the veil, He is coming.
You don't need to fear either door—because Jesus stands on the other side of both.

Door One: The Savior's Return

Jesus didn't say "I might come back."
He said, "I will come again and receive you to Myself, that where I am, you may be also." (John 14:3)

That was a promise, not poetry. And when He makes a promise, Heaven writes it in stone. There is a day—set, sealed, and soon—when the skies will split open. The trumpet will sound. The dead in Christ will rise first. And then you—you who know Him, love Him, walk with Me—you'll be caught up in the air to meet Him.

You'll feel it before your mind catches up. A tug deep in your spirit. A quickening in your bones. Your body will change— glorious, weightless, whole. Your thoughts will clear like morning fog burning off the hills. And as the world gasps, you'll rise. Higher and higher.

Then you'll see Him—Jesus. Face bright like the sun. Smile soaked in joy. And His eyes—an ocean of love—locked on you. This isn't a fairy tale or wishful thinking. This is the promise He made, and the promise He keeps.

So be encouraged, and let this truth anchor your hope: Jesus is coming back, and He will collect what He paid for—you.

Scripture Anchor:
"...we are citizens of heaven, where the Lord Jesus Christ lives. And we are eagerly waiting for him to return... He will take our weak mortal bodies and change them into glorious bodies like his own..." (Philippians 3:20–21)

Door Two: Death — The Quiet Crossing

But maybe your journey in this world ends before His return. Maybe your finish line comes sooner. Even so—He is still coming for you. Because death isn't defeat. It's a doorway into God's presence: to your Father, to your Savior... and yes, you'll even see Me in ways you can't imagine.

That last breath on earth will be your first inhale of Heaven. You'll blink—and Jesus will be standing before you. Not with pity, but with joy. Not with questions, but with His nail-pierced hand extended, ready to lead you to your Father.

And just like that, this broken shell will fall away. And you'll be free. No more pain. No more fear. No more sorrow. Just God. Just love. Just Home.

Scripture Anchor:
"He will wipe away every tear from their eyes, and death shall be no more... neither shall there be mourning, nor crying, nor pain anymore, for the former things have passed away." (Revelation 21:4)

The Same Love Stands Behind Both Doors

There's no need to obsess over which door it will be. Both doors open to the same eternity. Both are bought by the same blood of Jesus. Plus, you're not in charge of the timing—He is. Your job is to trust Him. Walk with Him. Stay ready. Stay close.

So, live with hope and purpose. And live like someone who knows eternity is coming... Because it is. And when it finally arrives... You won't be afraid. You'll be home.

Scripture Anchor:
"...while we wait for the blessed hope—the appearing of the glory of our great God and Savior, Jesus Christ." (Titus 2:13)

Life Without Limits
(What Eternity Really Feels Like)

You've heard the jokes, haven't you?
White robes. Endless harp practice. Floating around like some ghostly choir member trying not to fall asleep mid-hymn.

Let Me be very clear: Heaven is NOT boring.

If you think God went wild with creativity on Earth—mountains, oceans, giraffes, galaxies—what do you think happens when He removes all limits? Every color, every sound, every expression of creativity, design, purpose, and joy will be beyond anything you've ever known—brilliant, overwhelming, more alive than anything on this side of eternity... And so will you.

Your gifts? Amplified. Your joy? Uncontainable. Your relationships? Pure and whole. Your worship? Deeper than any song and woven into every breath. No clocks, no pressure, no fear—just you, fully known and fully loved by God, moving in perfect rhythm with your Father, with your Savior... with Me, exactly the way it was always meant to be.

Scripture Anchor:
"No eye has seen, no ear has heard, no mind has conceived what God has prepared for those who love him."
(1 Corinthians 2:9)

Forever Fellowship
(Family the Way it Was Supposed to Be)

Think about the best fellowship you've ever experienced: A warm hug from a grandparent. A moment of meaningful encouragement from a parent or mentor. A deep, tear-streaming, belly-aching laugh with a friend who gets you.

Now... multiply that by infinity—and you still won't touch what fellowship feels like in eternity.

There will be no pride. No insecurity. No comparison or competition. You won't shrink yourself to feel accepted, and no one will elevate themselves to feel important. Every relationship will be pure—healed.

You'll celebrate others without feeling smaller. You'll be celebrated without feeling guilty. No tension, no secrets, no fear. Just real soul-deep connection in the presence of God.

Scripture Anchor:
"Dear friends, now we are children of God, and what we will be has not yet been made known. But we know that when Christ appears, we shall be like him, for we shall see him as he is." (1 John 3:2)

Scripture Anchor:
"I have given them the glory you gave me, so they may be one as we are one." (John 17:22)

Points to Ponder

- Am I living like someone who believes Jesus is coming back?

- Do I fear death—or trust the One who already conquered it?

- What distractions are pulling my heart away from the hope of Heaven?

- In what ways can I invite the fellowship of eternity into my relationships now?

- How can I let the promise of forever reshape how I face today?

Let's Bring It In

Eternity isn't a concept—it's a promise. Jesus meant it when He said He's coming to get you, one way or another. He promised... and because He cannot lie, you can bet your life on it. And what waits on the other side isn't just gold streets or angel choirs—it's life. Real life. Full-color, no-pain, never-ending life.

You'll know peace like you've never known. You'll walk in purpose without pressure. You'll be surrounded by love that never fades and never fails. You'll be Home.

Princess, this is your future. Live like you believe it.

12
Final Letter

So here we are. The final page. You've made it through lessons on everything from dating to spiritual warfare, hormones to health, heartbreak to healing. You've been challenged to grow in the Word, to pray like it matters (because it does), to guard your purity, to trust The King when it hurts, and to rise with integrity when The Dragon knocks you down.

And now, before you step out into the wild world of Dystopia, there's one more thing I need you to hear. Something I've been trying to show you this whole time...

You are not alone.

The King of Lights has never stopped watching over you, and the Savior (Jesus, your White Knight) has never stopped interceding, washing, and loving you—not for a second.

And neither have I. Remember, I am the Helper. My job isn't to make the road easy—it's to walk it with you. To whisper truth when lies get loud. To remind you who you are when the fog rolls in.

This journey hasn't been about behavior correction or rule-following. It's been about awakening the princess inside you—who you were always meant to be.

You've been asleep for a long time, yes. But now your eyes are open. Darkness doesn't define you anymore. That dragon doesn't own you. And your shame? It's already been paid for. Your Father is waiting for you, Princess. In fact, He's preparing a celebration for your return—one that makes Cinderella's little ball look forgettable.

Robes. Crowns. Trumpets. Light.

But listen closely: the world will still try to lull you back to sleep. It will dress up lies as truth and call emptiness "freedom." Dystopia is tricky like that. But you, my dear, are not without direction. You have the map. You have the sword. You have the armor. You have the truth. And most importantly—you have Him, Princess.

You are The King's daughter. You carry His light inside you, and the world—this messy, broken world—needs it. You might feel small or insignificant, but let me tell you a secret: even the tiniest light can shatter the deepest darkness.

So shine, Princess. Walk in the truth of who you are.
Love boldly. Live bravely. And never, ever forget this:
You are saved by the blood of Jesus.
Chosen by your Father—the King.
And loved completely and eternally.

Keep your eyes on The Way Road. Let no detour tempt you.
If you fall, get up. If you're tired, lean on Me.
I'll be with you every step of the way home.
Always.

Sincerely,
The Helper

ABOUT THE AUTHOR

JESSICA GALAXY is a writer of stories for children and tweens—tales that sparkle with hope, wrestle with truth, and invite young hearts to dream a little bigger. Her words are for the wildflowers, the dandelion kids, and the ones who wonder if they still belong in the story. (Spoiler: they do.) She believes in crowns even when they're crooked, in light that sneaks through the cracks, and in the quiet courage it takes to stand—even when you have to balance on shaky knees.

Her books are soaked in Scripture, stitched with wonder, and woven with reminders that even the smallest voice can make a difference.

When she's not writing, you can find her drinking tea with her daughters, talking to Jesus like He's in the room (because He is), or wandering down The Way Road in search of the next story.

Jessica Galaxy is a part of Wayfolk Press, a fellowship of story keepers and soul stirrers devoted to sacred psalms, knitted prayers, and the kind of tales that linger long after the last page is turned. It's less of a company, more of a lantern-lit table—where creative minds gather like old friends, trade ink-soaked mysteries and speak light into the darkness.

You can follow her journey or discover more stories at:
www.WayfolkPress.com
or on Instagram @WayfolkPress

www.ingramcontent.com/pod-product-compliance
Lightning Source LLC
Chambersburg PA
CBHW061735120626
46550CB00005B/1803